CREATED
IN THE IMAGE
OF GOD

*Scripture tells us that we are designed
for a better lifestyle*

John Brooks

Discern Products
Ottawa
2016

Cover design is by D.V. Suresh

Published by Discern Products
724 Parkdale Avenue
Ottawa, Ontario Canada K1Y 1J6
info@discernproducts.com

Library and Archives of Canada Cataloguing in Publication is available upon request.

ISBN 978-0-96800-612-2

Printed in Canada

To my wife, Brenda

CONTENTS

THE GREAT SOCIAL EXPERIMENT

"For my thoughts are not your thoughts,
neither are your ways my ways,' declares the Lord"
(Isaiah 55:8).

Richard Clarke Cabot of Harvard University began perhaps the most ambitious formal social scientific experiment ever conducted. He set out to prove potentially delinquent boys from poor neighborhoods could be transformed if they enjoyed the social benefits of the middle class. He offered a program of kindness.

The social climate of 1935 was much different than today. Social Darwinism was the popular theory used to justify a lack of social supports. The belief was that "survival of the fittest" would lead to a stronger society and thus the theory questioned efforts to prop up the less fortunate. Prejudice and racism were simply the way of life.

This great social experiment appeared to have the ideal leader in Cabot. The experiment would be done properly because he was one of the leading scientists of the day. His discoveries included Cabot rings (a structure in certain blood cells), the Cabot-Locke murmur (a heart symptom he showed was due to anemia instead of faulty heart valves as previously thought) and how to differentiate typhoid fever from malaria.

Cabot possessed a strong spiritual and social side as well. He was a practicing Christian who believed in helping others. He hired Garnet Pelton as a social worker to help hospital patients in need. Pelton is recognized as the first professional social worker in the United States. Since the hospital refused to pay her salary, Cabot paid it out of his own pocket. Later, he became president of the National Conference of Social Work.

A sound experiment requires a large number of participants so the results are statistically valid. For example, a poll of 3,000 participants is statistically more accurate than one with 30 participants. A large sample would be very expensive, but Cabot arranged the funding and the Cambridge-Somerville Youth Study was born. His team recruited 650 underprivileged boys around the age of ten who were considered potential delinquents. Half got social support while the other half got nothing, making them a control group.

The boys who got support received virtually everything that Cabot could imagine. Each had a personal counselor who met with the boys and their families to determine needs. The counselors followed up at least twice a month. The boys had academic tutoring, recreational activities and summer camps. Their families were helped through interventions like day care arrangements and employment assistance. Any problem that developed was addressed.

The program was believed to be effective until a 30-year follow-up study revealed that it was one of the most dramatic failures ever in social science research.[1] In the words of Timothy Wilson of the University of Virginia "the men who had been in the treatment were *more* likely to have died at a young age, *more* likely to have committed repeated crimes, *more* likely to show signs of alcoholism and *more* likely to have had serious mental illnesses than were the men in the control condition."[2]

The failure shows that good intentions are not enough. The men retained an image of themselves as inferior people and this ultimately caused havoc in most of their lives. Imagine the contrast with the understanding that we are created in the image of God. Through identifying ourselves as His children and developing ourselves in His image, we will "receive many times as much in this age, and in the age to come, eternal life" (Luke 18:30).

In this book, we will explore how Scripture tells us to flourish on earth and the supporting evidence behind this from both a Biblical and a scientific perspective. Flourishing means that the Christian lifestyle is more successful, meaningful, healthier and happier than the secular lifestyle. This statement is in stark contrast to the common understanding that Christians are called for a life of sacrifice in hope of eternal rewards.

Part One of the book will discuss how we create an identity in the Image of God, why it is important and the barriers Satan has to hold us back. Then Part Two looks at what a flourishing life is like living in the image of God. Finally, Part Three ties in important emotions related to our happiness, our motivation and dealing with our troubles.

C.S. Lewis wrote: "If there lurks in most modern minds the notion that to desire our own good and earnestly to hope for the enjoyment of it is a bad thing, I submit that this notion has crept in from Kant and the Stoics and is not part of the Christian faith. Indeed, if we consider the unblushing promises of reward and the staggering nature of the rewards promised in the Gospels, it would seem that Our Lord finds our desires not to be too strong, but too weak.[3] Lewis documents how unexpected joy guided his study as he went from atheism to Christianity.[4]

Like Lewis and many others have found, a detailed examination of the evidence inevitably leads us to believing in Jesus and accepting His Word. So, let's look at how the Bible guides us to a better life on earth through growth in the image of God.

Part 1

IDENTIFYING WITH GOD

CHAPTER ONE

LOVE GOD

"Jesus replied: 'Love the Lord your God with all your heart and with all your soul and with all your mind. This is the first and greatest commandment'"

(Matthew 22:37-38).

When Jesus gives us a commandment, as believers we feel that we must follow it. Since it is the greatest commandment, it becomes the greatest obligation. If we interpret this commandment as the first rule in a rulebook, we will feel inadequate because we will never be able to do enough. A better idea is to consider these words of Jesus as a great gift that will lead to an easier, happier and more productive life. We can sense this is true because we know that He loves us.

The Meaning of Love

The word love is generally used to describe a feeling filled with happiness. This type of love comes from our heart and can't be commanded. So, this is not what Jesus means when he commands us to love God. Although this is not the command, it does not preclude us from eventually developing this type of emotional love toward God. As we develop our relationship with Jesus, it is a natural consequence of our growth.

A common misinterpretation of this commandment is that it is a call for us to worship God. Indeed, we are called to worship, but

God did not create us because He wanted a billion people to worship Him and feed His ego. John Piper writes: "The one who actually sets himself above God is the person who presumes to come to God to give rather than get. With a pretense of self-denial, he positions himself as God's benefactor."[1] Worship is vital and the reasons will be discussed in Chapter 5, yet is not the all encompassing love called for in His greatest commandment.

The answer to the dilemma is found in the meaning of the word "love." Many Christians assume that this means the unconditional love found in the Bible that describes God's love for us or perhaps the love a mother may have for her infant, but this is incorrect. The Greek word used in the original text, *agapao*, is also used for a self-centered type of love.

Most children love ice cream. The *agapao* love called for in the greatest commandment is that type of love where we want something rather than the love where we desire to give of ourselves. It is a commitment such that our identity becomes tied up in whatever we love. Your identity can be tied up in many avenues other than God such as wealth, recognition, career, physical appearance or pleasures. Some examples follow where the word *agapao* is used in the Bible as a self-centered love of what we want:

- "Even sinners love those who love them" (Luke 6:32)
- "Woe to you Pharisees, because you love the most important seats in the synagogues" (Luke 11:43)
- "People loved darkness instead of light because their deeds were evil" (John 3:19)
- "They loved human praise more than praise from God" (John 12:43)
- "Demas, because he loved the world, has deserted me" (2 Timothy 4:10)
- "If anyone loves the world, love for the Father is not in them" (1 John 2:15)

The greatest commandment calls on us to develop ourselves in His image. We will never reach the power and perfection of God, but accepting His commandment is a life changing experience. Think of a parent with a young child. Does the parent prefer praise from the child or for the child to develop according to his or her strengths? In the same way, we are children of God and He wants us to mature in His image more than He wants us to praise Him.

Changing ourselves holds us to a much higher standard than performing an activity and it is not obvious where to start. We understand how to take actions like worshiping, obeying or helping someone in need, but changing our minds is more difficult. And where would we start to change our hearts? For guidance, let's draw upon perhaps the greatest Biblical scholar of all time, Augustine of Hippo.

Augustine of Hippo

Augustine is respected as a teacher across Christian churches more than anyone else other than some teachers who lived at the time of Jesus. (C.S. Lewis is probably a distant second). He had an advantage in that he lived in the Roman Empire and thus was better able to appreciate the nuances that Scripture intended, especially the New Testament which was written at a time close to when he lived.

He put considerable effort into understanding what it means to be created in the image of God because he felt that this was important in drawing him closer to God. Before we look at his teaching, consider how other Christian leaders have viewed Augustine:

John Wesley: "St. Augustine was then in the Christian world, what Aristotle was afterwards: There needed no other proof of any assertion, than *Ipse dixit*: 'St. Augustine said it.'"[2]

Martin Luther: "Augustine was the ablest and purest of all the doctors."[3]

John Calvin: "[Augustine is the one] we quote most frequently as being the best and most faithful witness of all antiquity."[4]

C.S. Lewis: "Augustine was theologically massive in Lewis's life. Read Augustine, and you'll better understand where Lewis's theological ideas stem from, especially his ideas concerning the trinity."[5]

Pope John Paul II: "It is well known how much Augustine loved Sacred Scripture, proclaiming its divine origin, its inerrancy, its depth and inexhaustible riches; and it is well known how much he studied Scripture." and "I too have added my voice to those of my predecessors [previous popes], when I expressed my strong desire that his [Augustine's] philosophical, theological and spiritual doctrine be studied and spread."[6]

The Growth of Augustine

Augustine of Hippo converted to Christianity in 386 and matured into one of the greatest leaders in Christian theology. The change in his prayers shows his development from seeking the joy of the secular world to finding the incredible joy that comes when we surrender our lives to Jesus. At first, he prayed "God grant me chastity, but not yet." Later in his life, he prayed a different type of prayer, one that shows that he found the spiritual beauty of truly knowing the peace of God is greater than the outward beauty of the world.

"Late have I loved you, O Beauty ever ancient, ever new, late have I loved you. In my unloveliness, I plunged into the lovely things which you created. You were with me, but I was not with you. Created things kept me from you; yet if they had not been in you they would have not been at all. You called, you broke through my deafness. You flashed, you shone, and you dispelled my blindness. You breathed your fragrance on me; I drew in breath and now I pant for you. I have tasted you, now I hunger and thirst for more. You touched me, and I burned for your peace."[7]

What it Means to Be Created in God's Image

Edmund Hill, the translator of Augustine's book *The Trinity*, wrote that Augustine was not simply explaining theology. For Augustine it was "an imperative, a program to be carried out in order to discover the mystery of the Trinity by achieving its likeness in oneself."[8] This overwhelming urge Augustine felt to understand how he was created in the image of God and then seek to transform himself back to that natural state has a clear basis in Scripture. We are "created to be like God in true righteousness and holiness" (Ephesians 4:24).

Augustine starts his analysis with the story of creation. He understood the verse "Then God said, 'Let us make mankind in Our image'" (Genesis 1:26) means that being created in the image of God is in the image of the Trinity, since "us" is pleural.[9] He then teaches the three components of the Trinity in which our minds are in the image of God are memory, understanding and love. "If anyone intelligently regards as by nature divinely appointed in his own mind, and remembers by memory, contemplates by understanding, embraces by love, how great a thing that is in the mind, whereby even the eternal and unchangeable nature can be recollected, beheld, desired, doubtless that man finds an image of that highest Trinity."[10]

Augustine associated memory as in the image of God the Father as the creator. Memories are what the mind creates. Our lives and the memories that we have created through them are valuable to us. Whenever you are responsible for something valuable, then there is a natural inclination to protect it. So it follows that a natural priority of our minds will be to obtain the basic needs required to maintain ourselves.

The second way Augustine taught that we are created in the image of God is our capacity for understanding. The understanding that Jesus taught us was a new way of thinking. The second priority of the mind is to think clearly and the best way we can do this is to follow the teachings of Jesus. "You are in Christ Jesus, who has become for us wisdom from God" (1 Corinthians 1:30).

Finally, as Augustine wrote: "the truth itself has persuaded us, that as no Christian doubts the Word of God to be the Son, so that the Holy Spirit is love."[11] Loving others, both in giving and receiving love, is the third natural priority. "God's love has been poured out into our hearts through the Holy Spirit, who has been given to us" (Romans 5:5).

The secular world may question if helping others is truly a priority of the mind, but hundreds of scientific studies confirm that we receive measurable health benefits from charity, so our minds must be created for altruism. For example, seniors were tested both in giving massages to infants and in receiving massages. In both cases, measurable health improvements were found, but giving a massage showed greater benefits than receiving one. The benefits measured were fewer stress hormones, less depression and lower anxiety.[12] "We must help the weak, remembering the words the Lord Jesus himself said: 'It is more blessed to give than to receive'" (Acts 20:35).

While Augustine did not specify the three natural priorities of the mind, they clearly flow from his teaching of how we are created in the image of the Trinity. Creation gives rise to seeking the resources to maintain our lives, understanding gives rise to thinking clearly and love leads to helping others.

At this point, it is reasonable to be skeptical about Augustine's understanding around the image of God and how it relates to the greatest commandment. Later in this book we will explore how this teaching is helpful in understanding the spiritual illusions we face and how it changes our understanding of the virtue of humility. We will also see how science backs up Augustine's work in the fields of happiness, motivation and trauma. The evidence indicates that Augustine is right and gives us helpful guidance in our daily life.

A full appreciation of what it means to be created in God's image is beyond our comprehension. Our understanding of God is described as "a poor reflection as in a mirror" (1 Corinthians 13:12). The simplification of God described by Augustine is useful in helping us transform our lives, so we should not be put off by the reality that there is more to God than we are able to grasp.

The Ultimate Relationship

Augustine writes: "This distinction, then, of the inseparable Trinity is not to be merely accepted in passing, but to be carefully considered; for hence it was that the Word of God was specially called also the Wisdom of God, although both the Father and Holy Spirit are wisdom. If, then, any one of the three is to be specially called Love, what more fitting than that it should be the Holy Spirit."[13] "It is the sounder thing both to believe and understand that the Holy Spirit is not alone in love in that Trinity, yet is not specially called love to no purpose."[14]

Whenever love exists, there must be the lover, the loved and the love itself. Augustine teaches, "And if the love by which the Father loves the Son, and the Son loves the Father, ineffably demonstrates the communion of both, what is more suitable than that He should be specially called love, who is the Spirit common to both?"[15] "The Holy Spirit, according to Holy Scriptures, is neither of the Father alone, nor of the Son alone, but of both; and so intimates to us a mutual love, wherewith the Father and the Son reciprocally love one another."[16]

The three persons of the "inseparable Trinity" are so close that they are one God. Our creation in the image of God means that we are also built for loving relationships in the image of the Holy Spirit.

Living in the Image of God

There may be other ways in which we are created in God's image, but it is hard to imagine any more important than these three. We are created and offered eternal life in the image of God the Father, understanding in the image of Jesus and love in the image of the Holy Spirit. We are truly blessed with the opportunity to live the Christian life.

Summary

Loving God with all our heart, soul and mind is a depth of love that goes far beyond the call to worship. It is a love where our identity is tied to God. That is the meaning of the of the Greek word "agapao" found in the greatest commandment, which has been translated into the word love.

Augustine sought to get close to God by understanding and then living in His image. Based on his detailed understanding of Scripture, he determined the image of God means creation in the image of God the Father, understanding in the image of Jesus and love in the image of the Holy Spirit. From this we can see that the three natural priorities of the mind are to meet our basic needs, to think clearly and to help others.

Later in this book, we will devote a chapter to each of the three natural priorities of the mind and then show how they can guide us to achieving happiness, motivating ourselves and coping with the problems we face. But before we go into them, we will explore the importance of accepting our identity in the image of God, the stumbling block preventing us from so and the three spiritual illusions that hinder our progress.

CHAPTER TWO

ACCEPT THE GLORY

"Count yourselves dead to sin but alive to God in Christ Jesus"
(Romans 6:11).

C hristians have interpreted the Bible with a comforting narrative around sin which is both dangerous and wrong. We have been told to identify as weak sinners, thereby embracing what we think is humility. However, our weakness is offset by a loving God who will quickly forgive our sins. And we are further comforted by the thought that we are all sinners, thereby minimizing our personal responsibility.

Forgiving sin is important, but forgiveness alone does not eliminate the damage the sin has done to our identity. This chapter will explore the danger in creating the sinful identity and examine what the Bible really says. Do you count yourself as a sinner or as a child of God who sometimes sins but is maturing in line with God's plan on His timeline?

Chapter 1 calls for the re-definition of what it means to love God. This chapter calls for changing your identity as a sinner. Chapter 3 then re-defines humility. All three of these are contrary to the way many Christians have been taught the faith. All call for prayerful reflection. Of the three, accepting the change to your identity as a sinner is the most difficult, but that is clearly what he Bible is calling for when it says "count yourself dead to sin."

Accept the Biblical Teaching on Sin and Self Image

When you truly give your entire mind to Jesus, then you can free yourself from the chains of sin. How you feel in your heart is the true essence of who you are and you need to feel righteous in order to be righteous. Reflect on these Scripture passages:

- "If you hold to my teachings, you are really my disciples. Then you will know the truth, and the truth will set you free....everyone who sins is a slave to sin" (John 8:31-34).

- When Jesus saved the woman from being stoned for adultery, his parting words to her were "Neither do I condemn you. Go now and leave your life of sin" (John 8:11).

- "No one who is born of God continues to sin, because God's seed remains in them; they cannot go on sinning, because they have been born of God. This is how we know who the children of God are and who the children of the devil are: Anyone who does not do what is right is not God's child; nor is anyone who does not love their brother and sister" (1 John 3:9-10).

- "In the same way, count yourselves dead to sin but alive to God in Christ Jesus" (Romans 6:11).

- "May God Himself, the God of peace, sanctify you through and through. May your whole spirit, soul and body be kept blameless at the coming of our Lord Jesus Christ" (1 Thessalonians 5:23).

- "You were taught, with regard to your former way of life, to put off your old self, which is being corrupted by its deceitful desires; to be made new in the attitude of your minds; and to put on the new self, created to be like God in true righteousness and holiness" (Ephesians 4:22-24).

The Stages of Moving Away from Sin

Fighting sin through willpower is difficult because the more we try, the greater will be the anticipated pleasure of the sin. As we will discuss in Chapter 4, it is an illusion that sin will bring us more joy. As human beings, we fall for the illusion and often indulge in a self-centered search for what we feel will bring us joy, either immediately or in the future. When we become Christians, our behavior and motivations change as we seek to follow Jesus. There are three stages in our quest to avoid sin. The more we come to know and embrace the teachings of Jesus, the more effective we will be in avoiding sin.

As newly initiated Christians, we often think doing good works will help us in heaven. We know the day of judgment is coming and God is a just judge. "Store up for yourselves treasures in heaven, where moths and vermin do not destroy, and where thieves do not break in and steal" (Matthew 6:20). So, we are seeking to find future joy when we refrain from sin. This approach is weak because it is based on avoiding human failings. The illusion that sin brings us more pleasure than avoiding sin is simply too powerful for us to overcome without God's help.

Unfortunately, seeking to deny sin makes it appear more attractive. For example, studies show that pornography use is higher in areas with a large number of Christians than in non-Christian areas.[1,2] We feel guilt and shame, but sin seems to win out over our uncomfortable feelings.

The second stage of thought involves avoiding sin because we realize that sin hurts God and sometimes other people as well. We begin to think more of loving and helping others and this love can be a powerful force. While it is good to go beyond selfish motives, we still remain a long way from living in the image of God. Think of this as an intermediate stage where we are still working on avoiding sin by using our willpower. "For I have the desire to do what is good, but I cannot carry it out. For I do not do the good I want to do, but the evil I do not want to do–this I keep on doing" (Romans 7:18-19).

As we grow in the knowledge of Christ, more joy and control over sin comes when we surrender our lives to Him.

"Come to me, all you who are weary and burdened, and I will give you rest. Take my yoke upon you and learn from me, for I am gentle and humble in heart, and you will find rest for your soul. For my yoke is easy and my burden is light" Matthew 11:28-30.

When we reach this advanced stage with the Holy Spirit supporting us from within, we simply lose interest in sin.

"Those who live according to the sinful nature have their minds set on what that nature desires; but those who live in accordance with the Spirit have their minds set on what the Spirit desires. The mind governed by the flesh is death, but the mind governed by the Spirit is life and peace" (Romans 8:5-6).

Christian joy is the comfort that comes through knowing about salvation and our eternal rewards–but that is barely the first taste. Full Christian joy involves a craving to know Jesus better and to love deeper and stronger. When we awake in the morning, we are energized towards a day full of seeking the joy that comes from love and growth.

This craving to know Jesus better is what Thomas Chalmers spoke about in his famous sermon "The expulsive power of a new affection". He said that a moralist that seeks to avoid sin because it is wrong will have quite limited success. Success over sin requires replacing our affection for sin with an affection for the Gospel.[3]

Recognize the Importance of Identity

We act according to what we believe is our natural inclination. For example, if we believe that we love animals, we will react with kindness towards animals without conscious thought. Scientists term this our self-schema, but we will use the common term identity. When we say identity, we are referring to how we view ourselves rather than how others view us.

In Chapter 4, we will explore the control illusion which talks about how our conscious thoughts are controlled by our hearts. The ten examples that follow may appear to be excessive, but we are fighting an illusion deeply engrained within our hearts and the stakes are extremely high. The greatest commandment calls for more than action, it calls for a change in your identity.

Billions of dollars have been wasted on programs that ignored the issue of identity. Attempting to change negative behavior by appealing to the intellect is doomed to failure if at the same time a negative identity is implanted into the heart. To illustrate the point, here are examples of programs that failed because the intellectual approach also fostered a negative identity.

Scared Straight into Crime

Inmates serving sentences of twenty-five or more years at the Rahway State Prison in New Jersey decided they wanted to help others avoid their mistakes. With the help of the prison superintendent, the local police chief and a juvenile court judge, the Juvenile Awareness Project was born. The shock of touring the prison was expected to deter high-risk teenagers from a life of crime. A documentary on the program won an Academy Award and it became the most popular new series in the history of the A&E network.

Various scientific studies have shown that programs such as Scared Straight actually increase the crime rate.[4] When Timothy Wilson at the University of Virginia analyzed various scientific studies on the program, he concluded that of the 50,000 kids who participated, an estimated 6,500 more turned to crime than if the program did not exist.[5]

The Multi-Billion Dollar D.A.R.E. that Did Not Work

Started in 1983 in Los Angeles, the D.A.R.E. program (Drug Abuse Resistance Education) used police officers to teach kids not only about the dangers of drug and alcohol abuse, but also how to resist peer pressure. It expanded to 75% of the school districts across the country as well as internationally to forty other countries.

Why was a program allowed to grow and spread before it was tested, wasting more than a billion dollars annually in the United States alone?[6] The program expanded quickly because it sought to address a major problem, appeared intellectually solid and received great testimonials. But it sent the wrong message to the kids because it labeled them as potential drug or alcohol abusers. D.A.R.E has now revamped their program to focus on teaching skills and reports encouraging results.[7]

How Do We Know if a Program Works?

A common way to test a program is to have the participants fill out feedback questionnaires. The false logic is that if the participants feel a program has benefitted them, then the program must be good. Unfortunately, this simple equation equals bad science.

To really understand if a program works, we need to randomly split the participants into two groups. Half receive the treatment and the other half serve as a control group. Then, we can compare the two groups to see if those treated fared any better than those without the treatment.

Some programs organizers were shocked when they undertook proper testing. For example, the Critical Incident Stress Debriefing is a program where someone exposed to a traumatic event discusses it in detail with a professional counsellor. It had a 98% positive rating on the feedback questionnaires. When the program was properly tested with police and firefighters, it did not work. Half of these emergency providers received the treatment when exposed to a trauma and the other half, randomly selected, received no treatment. Those who received treatment reported more post-traumatic stress disorder and missed more time from work than those left untreated.[8]

Even a Program of Kindness Fails

As we saw in the introduction, the Cambridge-Somerville Youth Study gave underprivileged boys the economic and social advantages of the middle class, yet this intervention based on kindness caused more harm than good. The program addressed their intellectual and physical needs, but failed to address how they felt about themselves.[9]

What the Anomaly Means to Christians

The reason why programs such as Scared Straight, D.A.R.E. and the Cambridge-Somerville Youth Study fail is that they take an intellectual approach that does not consider how the kids feel about themselves. When they are labeled as potential criminals, potential drug users or potential delinquents, they tend to behave like the labels indicate.

The image we have of ourselves shapes our behavior. This is why it is vital we recognize that we are created in the image of God. When we receive the Holy Spirit, we are on the path to restoring the glory in our hearts.

Programs that Address Identity Work

Programs work that provide a positive identity in addition to useful support and information. The Nurse-Family Partnership Program is an example that has been proven effective through multiple scientific studies. The program reduces child abuse, reduces juvenile crime and improves a child's readiness to enter school. First-time mothers are given sixty-four planned home visits over a two-and-a-half-year period.

The program is about relationships as much as it is about giving information on how to care for an infant. The relationship between the nurse and the mother is what leads to the information being used effectively. The nurse fosters self-efficacy in the mother and helps the mother within her social context. The reason that it is successful is that it addresses the heart as well as the intellect.[10]

The Identity You Encourage Will Win

"Two natures beat within my breast
The one is cursed, the other blessed
The one I love, the other I hate
The one I feed will dominate"
        -attributed to an unknown US Marine

An elderly Cherokee Native American was teaching his grandchildren about life...He said to them, "A fight is going on inside me, it is a terrible fight and it is between two wolves. One wolf is evil -- he is fear, anger, envy, sorrow, regret, greed, arrogance, self-pity, guilt, resentment, inferiority, lies, false pride, competition, superiority, and ego. The other is good---he is joy, peace, love, hope, sharing, serenity, humility, kindness, benevolence, friendship, empathy, generosity, truth, compassion and faith. This same fight is going on inside you, and inside every other person, too." They thought about it for a minute and then one child asked his grandfather, "Which wolf will win?" The old Cherokee simply replied: "The one you feed". -a disputed Cherokee legend

The actual origin of this inspirational idea is unclear. The earliest printed reference appears to be John Bisagno's book The Power of Positive Praying (1965)[11.] Billy Graham repeated it in his book The Holy Spirit, Activating God's Power in Your Life (1978)[12]. It has also been in movies such as "The Missing" (2003) and "Pathfinder" (2007).

Small Cues Shape our Identity

An experiment at Stanford University was done with children in the second grade to test how their attitudes developed. A child was brought into a room with many interesting toys. For half the children, the researcher said that he was going out of the room for a few minutes and told them "you can play with all of the toys except the robot, and if you play with it, I will be very upset and very angry with you." For the other half, the researcher used the words "a little bit annoyed" instead of "very upset and very angry". Both the strong threat and the potential minor annoyance stopped all of the children from playing with the robot.

The reason for not playing with the robot was, of course, quite different between the two groups. Those with the strong threat did it to avoid punishment while the others told themselves that they were good people. A simple act of being good without the threat of punishment led to an identity of being a good person.

What was most revealing was that the identity carried over to a second test done three weeks later with a different researcher. The children were told that if they could accumulate a score of 35 on an electronic bowling game, they would get a nice prize. The test was to see if the kids would lie about their score since the game was rigged to shut off at 33 points. Very few of the kids who had the positive identity lied to get the prize, whereas a substantial number of those who were given the severe threat three weeks earlier chose to lie when they were asked about their score.[13]

Before we dismiss the experiment as applying just to kids, consider a study that duplicated the finding with college students. College students were manipulated either into thinking they were good or that they avoided cheating because of a threat. On a test a week later, those who were threatened cheated four times as much as those in the group who had developed a good identity during the earlier experiment.[14]

More Examples of the Heart Sabotaging the Intellect

Our intellect incorrectly believes that the decisions we make are based on the circumstances before us and that unconscious feelings

22

we have regarding our identity are not considered. Often identity should have no bearing on the decision, yet it still exerts a powerful influence. Here are more examples that demonstrate this fact about our nature:

Women were given a driving test with a simulator. One group was told that they were investigating why men are better drivers than women. The other group took the test without any mention of gender differences. Those that were told women are inferior drivers were more than twice as likely to hit a pedestrian.[15]

Another gender example applies to math. Girls in the United States are often told that boys have a better aptitude for math, so girls tend get poorer results in math than boys. When math aptitude is measured around the world, no gender difference exists. The idea that boys are somehow genetically superior in math is a myth, but the effects on identity are real.[16]

African-American students suffer from the stereotype that their IQ is lower as a group than whites. A study done with puzzles showed that blacks and whites were statistically equal when they were told that they were doing puzzles. But when the testing was done with other students who were told that it was an IQ test, then the blacks did significantly worse than the whites.[17]

A stereotype exists about older people being forgetful. So seniors do worse on memory tests if they are told the test is looking at age-related memory ability than if they are not told that it is an age-related test.[18]

For the final example, an experiment at Yale with subliminal perception showed the effect is truly coming from the heart. A group of 100 elderly participants, average age of 81, had words such as "spry" and "creative" flashed on a computer screen at speeds too fat to allow for conscious awareness. Simply placing these words into the unconscious minds of the participants brought about significant mental and physical benefits compared to the control participants.[19]

The important point to recognize from these studies is that we are often not aware of the strong effect our identity is having on our behavior. Our intellect is not in full control and never will be in our lifetimes. Paul wrote about this when he described his life before receiving the Holy Spirit: "it is no longer I who do it, but it is sin living in me that does it" (Romans 7:20).

Summary

In the first chapter, we saw that to love God means to identify with Him as we are created in His image. This chapter discusses the Biblical backing for the identity as a righteous person (who occasionally sins but is maturing according to God's timeline) and the evidence of why it is vital to have a positive identity.

The chapter looks at major programs that failed because they did not address the issue of identity. It also explores how our behavior will change if simple suggestions are made that remind us about part of our identity.

Scripture is clear in multiple places about the identity we are called to adopt, which is that of a righteous person. We are reluctant to do so because this appears to contradict what we have been taught humility means. So in the next chapter we will address the true meaning of humility in the image of God.

CHAPTER THREE

SATAN'S GREAT LIE

"Each one should test their own actions. Then they can take
pride in themselves, without comparing themselves to someone else"
(Galatians 6:4).

S atan's great lie is that we are not like God. It is even more powerful than his three spiritual illusions discussed in the next chapter because it strikes at our identity rather than at the priorities of our mind.

Satan misleads us so that we don't assume our rightful identity in the image of God. This deception shows up through a misunderstanding of the call to humility. There have been some good Christian teachings on what humility means but these teachings are incomplete if they lack the three ways Scripture calls for humility.

Augustine wrote "There is, therefore, something in humility which strangely enough exalts the heart, and something in pride which debases it. This seems to be contradictory, that loftiness debase and lowliness exalt."[1] So, let's examine the type of humility that exalts the heart.

Humility is destructive when it is defined as putting yourself down, either in your own mind or in front of others. Instead it should be defined as not comparing yourself to others, keeping an open mind and accepting your role as a servant to all. And the Bible teaches that pride should not always be defined as wrong, because it is valuable in some circumstances.

The 1959 classic film, A Nun's Story starring Audrey Hepburn, illustrates an extreme example of the common Christian understanding of humility. She was the top student in her class studying to be a nurse missionary in the Congo. Her success was viewed as interfering with her learning humility. The Mother Superior even instructed her to intentionally fail her exam to learn humility. This failure meant she could not go to serve the poor in Africa. Clearly, the idea that we should limit accomplishments that will help in doing God's Will for the sake of humility is wrong.

False Humility

False humility means putting ourselves down and is contrary to what the Bible teaches. When Jesus tells us "Take my yoke upon you and learn from me, for I am gentle and humble of heart" (Matthew 11:29), He is obviously not saying give me your troubles because I am not very good at dealing with them. Rather, he is saying that He can do more because of His humility.

There are two problems with false humility. The first, as we have discussed in the last chapter, is that we tend to do more of whatever we accept as our identity. So if our identity is as a sinner, our heart will prompt us to sin more. The second problem is that we substitute this incorrect version of humility for true humility that we need.

C.S. Lewis gives this humorous and insightful discussion with a senior devil teaching his young protégé:

> "You must therefore conceal from the patient the true end of humility. Let him think of it not as self-forgetfulness but as a certain kind of opinion (namely a low opinion) of his own talents and character. Some talents, I gather, he really has. Fix in his mind the idea that humility consists in trying to believe those talents to be less valuable than he believes them to be. No doubt they are in fact less valuable than he believes, but that is not the point. The great thing is to make

him value an opinion for some quality other than truth, thus introducing an element of dishonesty and make-believe into the heart of what otherwise threatens to become a virtue. By this method, thousands of humans have been brought to think that humility means pretty women trying to believe they are ugly and clever men trying to believe they are fools. And since what they are trying to believe may, in some cases, be manifest nonsense, they cannot succeed in believing it and we have the chance to keeping their minds endlessly revolving on themselves in an effort to achieve the impossible.[2]

Pride Can Be Good

It is human nature to strive to accomplish things. We feel joy when we achieve victories in accordance with God's Will. To diminish the joy of achievement is neither appropriate nor productive.

Many Christians fall victim to misunderstandings about pride and humility. So let us discard the simplistic notion that humility is the opposite of pride and take a closer look at what Scripture says. The Bible gives deep insights on this important topic.

Scripture is full of passages warning us about pride. "When pride comes, then comes disgrace, but with humility comes wisdom" (Proverbs 11:2). We learn that "God opposes the proud but shows favor to the humble" (James 4:6). It is easy to quickly condemn pride because "Pride goes before destruction, a haughty spirit before a fall" (Proverbs 16:18).

Yet the Bible also talks about pride in a positive fashion. We are instructed to take pride in ourselves. "Each one should test their own actions. Then they can take pride in themselves alone, without comparing themselves to somebody else" (Galatians 6:4). The Greek word used for this type of pride, *kauchema*, is found nine more times in the Bible. It is translated as boasting in Jesus (Philippians 2:16), other boasting (Romans 4:2, 1 Corinthians 5:6, 9:15, 9:16 and 2 Corinthians 1:14, 9:3), pride (2 Corinthians 5:12) and glory (Hebrews 3:6). So it is a strong feeling of pride that the Bible calls us to adopt.

This Biblical inspired pride is narrowly defined and controlled with a detailed understanding of humility. If we have no pride, we then are prone to lose our self-respect, to lapse into insecurity and to engage in self-pity. We should be proud of being created in the image of God and growing deeper within His image. At the same time, we must keep our pride in perspective. Just as the New Testament has far more verses teaching us to identify as righteous than as a sinner, we also see far more verses warning us against pride than encouraging it.

Humility in the Image of God the Father

The natural priority of the mind related to our identity in the image of God the Father is to meet the basic needs to maintain our life and achieve God's purpose for our lives. When we stop comparing ourselves to others, then we no longer have any desire to acquire things beyond our basic needs. So humility in the image of God the Father involves not comparing ourselves to others.

As we saw in Galatians 6:4, the pride we should take in ourselves is without comparing ourselves to others. Jesus was critical of the Pharisee who said "God, I thank you that I am not like other men–robbers, evildoers, adulterers–or even like this tax collector" (Luke 18:11). It is simply not our place to judge others and especially wrong to hold ourselves up as being better.

We are all created with different abilities and needs. So what would the point be of comparing ourselves to someone that God has chosen to create in a different manner? And when we consider ourselves better or inferior to someone, this inevitably affects the way we relate to that person.

Once we stop comparing ourselves to others, then it is easier to identify and accept our weaknesses because pride does not get in our way. "Each should test their own actions" (Galatians 6:4) and when we do so we will find areas to improve. At the same time, we should remain mindful that whatever these weaknesses are, they pale in comparison to our being created in the image of God.

Situations will arise when comparisons to others are inevitable, for instance as during a competition. We are not called to avoid competitions, to refrain from trying our hardest to be successful nor to reject the pleasure we feel from success. When we are working towards God's purpose for our lives, success should be a joyful feeling. However, we must be careful not to consider ourselves better than others.

A great benefit of not comparing ourselves to others is losing the desire for personal recognition. "There is no limit to what can be accomplished if it doesn't matter who gets the credit" (attributed to Ralph Waldo Emerson). Sometimes some personal recognition is needed to achieve God's purpose for our lives. When this happens, accept graciously without gloating. If possible, give the credit to God.

A sports analogy illustrates the role of humility and shows how it involves losing our personal objectives for the good of the team. Consider the situation where you are playing basketball and you are approaching the basket with a teammate. The decision of shooting the ball or passing it to a teammate rests solely on who has the best chance to score. At that instant, you do not consider the recognition you will get if you score. Rather, your personal objectives are secondary to team needs. Afterwards, we may revert to a personal agenda, but during that moment, we act in the true spirit of humility.

Science confirms the biblical wisdom of not comparing yourself to others. At the start of an experiment, half the participants were instructed to engage their mind in comparisons by focusing on their social class ranking in terms of income, education and job status. The researchers found that judging where you are relative to others led to a significant increase in unethical behavior.[3]

People who suffer from pride base their actions on what others will think of them. Humility allows you to go forward without being hindered by your pride.

Humility in Leadership

In his book, Good to Great, Jim Collins analyzed companies that transitioned into greatness. Using the Fortune 500 list, he examined 1,435 of the largest public companies in the US from 1965 to 1995. He sought companies that had started as average performers and then transitioned into greatness for at least fifteen years. Greatness was defined as at least three times better stock prices than average. Companies whose stock rose along with its specific industry were excluded. Eleven companies met the criteria.

The companies that made the list were Abbott, Circuit City, Fannie Mae, Gillette, Kimberly-Clark, Kroger, Nucor, Philip Morris, Pitney Bowes, Walgreens and Wells Fargo. When he and his team looked at why these eleven companies surged ahead of their peers, leadership came forward as making the difference. Collins initially asked his team to ignore the executive leadership as the reason for greatness, but eventually the data showed that leadership made the difference and the CEOs all shared similar traits.

Even though some companies on the list have now fallen on hard times under different leadership, his analysis is still valid. Collins termed the humility exhibited by the CEOs of these companies as Level 5 leadership. What is remarkable about these CEOs is that their names were virtually never in the press. They acted with a quiet resolve to get the job done, no matter how difficult. Then they gave the credit to others.[4]

Humility in the Image of Jesus

"With humility comes wisdom" (Proverbs 11:2). The second natural priority of the mind is to think clearly and to progress in this area we need an open mind. "Those who think they know something do not yet know as they ought to know" (1 Corinthians 8:2). To accept the Biblical call for continued growth in our understanding is harder than it appears.

When Jesus said "Go and make disciples of all nations" (Matthew 28:19), He used the word for disciples rather than followers, believers, supporters or worshippers. The Greek word is *manthetes* and it means students. The Greek text uses *manthetes* 194 times in the gospels, so it is clear that we are called to be His students. We stop being disciples of Jesus if we stop seeking to grow in our knowledge of His teachings. "Like newborn babies, crave pure spiritual milk, so that you may grow up in your salvation" (1 Peter 2:2).

Most people believe that they have a growth mindset rather than fixed mindset until they realize what this really means. Here are some examples to illustrate the difference.

- Do you believe the intelligence you have is inherited (fixed) or something you can develop (growth)? People with a growth mindset try to improve their intelligence.

- At the end of a game, are you more concerned with if you won (fixed) or how you played (growth)?

- Would you rather have your spouse or best friend praise you (fixed) or point out a flaw for you to work on (growth)?

- If you try hard to achieve a goal but are unable to accomplish it, do you consider yourself to have failed (fixed) or succeeded because of your effort and what you learned (growth)?

- When you think of Jesus, is the primary focus on the past (fixed) or on how He can help you become a better Christian (growth)?

31

Effective living with an open mindset requires an expansion of your critical thinking rather than simply accepting new ideas. For example, in reading this book, any concepts that could be helpful to your daily life should be investigated for flaws and then if the idea still appears helpful, it can be implemented. Study is part of the process to incorporate an idea into your heart.

Humility in the Image of the Holy Spirit

Humility allows us to feel our lives are worthwhile through service to others. And when we remove the mask pride puts on our face, we can relate to people in a deep and honest way. Humility is a key element in love, the third natural priority of the mind.

Humility in the image of the Holy Spirit is acceptance of our role as servants. At the last supper, Jesus washed the feet of the apostles to demonstrate the importance of becoming a servant. He said to them "The greatest of you should be like the youngest, and the one who rules like the one who serves. For who is greater, the one who is at the table or the one who serves? Is it not the one who is at the table? But I am among you as one who serves" (Luke 22:26-27). We are the children of God who serve Him.

Gary Chapman, the author of the bestselling book, The Five Love Languages, talks about his struggles early in his marriage to Karolyn. They married as he was completing his graduate degree in theology. Soon the loving marriage fell to arguing or suffering in silence. Gary questioned if he married the right person and also if he was suitable to be a minister since he could not manage his own marriage. He even got mad at God because his prayers seemed to make no difference. Karolyn would simply not listen to him as to how to fix their marriage. Gary felt he knew the answers and Karolyn was the problem.

Finally, Gary turned to God in a spirit of humility. Then his answer came in the form of a reference to Jesus taking the humble task of washing his disciples' feet at the last supper. Gary saw that he was being called to play the servant rather than master in the marriage. His change involved asking Karolyn three questions each day: What can I do for you today, how can I make your life easier and how can I be a better husband? The change was not instant. However, after a couple of months, the marriage was saved and 40 years later he said that they have an incredible relationship.[5]

Look at what Paul writes about service with humility:

"Do nothing out of selfish ambition or vain conceit. Rather in humility value others above yourselves, not looking at your own interests but each of you to the interests of the others. In your relationships with one another, have the same mindset as Christ Jesus: Who, being in very nature God, did not consider equality with God something to be used to His advantage, but made Himself nothing, taking the very nature of a servant, being made in human likeness" (Philippians 2:3-7).

C.S. Lewis said "Humility is not thinking less of yourself; it is thinking of yourself less"[6] and Rick Warren followed up on the quote with: "Humility is thinking more of others. Humble people are so focused on serving others, they don't think about themselves."[6]

Summary

True humility allows us to avoid the sins that come from pride. Humility also allows us to live in alignment with the three basic priorities of the mind, which are to meet our basic needs, to think clearly and to love. The false humility we encounter when we put ourselves down is ineffective.

Humility is not selling yourself short. Instead, it means that you do not compare yourself to others, you keep an open mind and you embrace your role as a servant to all. If you maintain this humility, Scripture calls you to take pride in yourself.

Satan knows your name and calls you by your sins. God knows your sins and calls you by your name. Your heart is listening to Satan so you identify as a sinner because then your heart will cause you to sin more. Yet this great lie is not Satan's only trick. Let's now explore the three illusions he uses to undermine our identity in the image of God.

CHAPTER FOUR

THE THREE ILLUSIONS

"The heart is deceitful above all things"
(Jeremiah 17:9).

T here have been thousands of religions, but it appears that only the Bible teaches about all three spiritual illusions. Since these illusions are counter-intuitive, this is further evidence that the Bible is the inspired Word of God. That is the only reasonable explanation for explaining how truths recently discovered by science could be found in a book 2000 years old.

Our path towards changing our identity to truly loving God is blocked by three powerful illusions, each relating to one of the three natural priorities of the mind based on our creation in the image of God. These illusions cause our intuition to differ from the truth. Recognizing how our hearts have been corrupted will not eliminate the corruption, but constant vigilance can limit the harm these illusions cause. If we recognize and focus on only one or two of them, then the third can destroy us.

The first natural priority of the mind is to meet our basic needs which brings pleasure, but it is an illusion to feel that more than what we need will bring us more pleasure. The second natural priority is to think clearly, but it is an illusion to feel that clear thought will eliminate the dominance of our hearts. Finally, the third natural priority is to help others, but it is an illusion to put our relationship with God on the same terms as our relationship with other people.

The Selfish Illusion

We will not be happier through seeking more than our basic needs. The Bible tells us this in the verse "put off your old self, which is being corrupted by its deceitful desires" (Ephesians 4:22). Deceitful desires are those that do not add to your happiness. Science confirm this teaching that living a meaningful life as Jesus taught brings true happiness, whereas trying to increase our happiness through materialism, hedonism or recognition is an illusion. God understands what makes us happy better than we do. Jesus told us that if we follow Him, we receive "many times as much in this age" (Luke 18:30). Yet, when we face daily situations, His Wisdom is often forgotten.

Our brains are wired in a zero-sum game such that if we get our pleasure from one source, then we feel less pleasure from another. From the neurological standpoint, it is called the mesolimbic dopaminergic reward system and means we are limited in the amount of the chemical dopamine that can be released to the brain. For example, a study looking at the chemical reactions in the brains of gambling addicts found that their ability to get the buzz of pleasure from situations unrelated to gambling was decreased.[1]

As if that is not enough, studies show that people who actively seek pleasure end up with less happiness than those who have other life goals.[2] The researchers give an example that someone who has a focus on an academic goal will achieve better academic results even if they do not accomplish their goal due to the effort they put in. However, trying to increase our pleasure not only fails because of the way our brains are wired, but then we also have the disappointment of our failed effort to deal with.

Abd Al-Rahman III was the absolute ruler of Spain in the tenth century. Here is how he wrote about his life: "I have now reigned above 50 years in victory or peace; beloved by my subjects, dreaded by my enemies and respected by my allies. Riches and honors, power and pleasure, have waited on my call, nor does any earthly blessing appear to have been wanting to my felicity. In this situation, I have diligently numbered the days of pure and genuine happiness which have fallen to my lot: They amount to fourteen."

The Control Illusion

The control illusion involves control over our minds rather than control over others as seen in the selfish illusion where we think power make us happier. We saw the control illusion in play in Chapter 2 where our identity controlled our actions. Augustine addressed the control illusion as he wrote "The mind commands the body, and it obeys: the mind commands itself, and it withstands"[3]

Even after we have accepted Jesus, we are still maturing and must face evil coming from our hearts. Paul taught about this when he wrote: "it is sin living in me that does it" (Romans 7:20). We are not even aware battle going on within our hearts, so we need the power of the Holy Spirit.

The control illusion opposes us accepting Jesus through faith since faith is not something we have full control over. It also inhibits our learning to trust Him because God works through our hearts and we can't see what is happening. We need God's grace to help us deal with the control illusion, which is freely available if we ask Him with an open mind.

When we believe that we control our lives, we then believe we have the power to control our sin. This leads to the vicious sin cycle where we seek to resist temptation through our willpower. This resistance makes the sin appear more attractive and we end up sinning even more. That leads to many negative consequences such as feeling shame, hiding secrets, pretending to be more righteous than we are, justifying behavior, blaming others or circumstances, withdrawing from others and in the end sometimes losing hope and falling into apathy.

In contrast to this sin cycle, consider what it means to you to have accepted Jesus. Consider a new life where the Holy Spirit controls your heart. This is part of trusting and receiving God's love. Then, you can accept that God is maturing you in His way according to His timeline and you are good with that.

Charles Darwin demonstrated the limit of his mind. He made the journey to the London Zoological Gardens to try a simple experiment with a snake from India called a Puff Adder. The walls of the terrarium where the snake made its home were made of thick, clear glass. Darwin stuck his face against the glass with a "firm determination of not starting back if the snake struck." He was testing the ability of his intellect to stay in control. He knew that he was in absolutely no danger because of the glass barrier; and because he had never been bitten by a snake, he was not suffering from the trauma of a bad snake experience.

Darwin writes, "As soon as the blow was struck, my resolution went for nothing, and I jumped a yard or two backward with astonishing rapidity. My will and reason were powerless against the imagination of a danger which had never been experienced." He had set up a confrontation between his intellect and his heart and his intellect clearly lost.[4]

The Reward Illusion

"For it is by grace that you have been saved through faith, and this is not from yourselves, it is the gift from God" (Ephesians 2:8). Christian teaching frequently talks about how we are saved by faith rather than by works, but neglects to tie the teaching into the strong bias we have for fairness. Consider what it means to come out and say that you will be unfair to God. It is easier to accept if we use the analogy that infants are unfair to their parents. Still it is hard to accept that you are unfair to the most important person in your life, Jesus Christ.

Our human logic tells us that our reward should be based on the sacrifice and suffering that we endure. Yet we can't even come close to meriting the grace God has given us based on our actions, so we need to put aside the notion of fairness. There is nothing we can do to make God love us more or to earn our salvation. "Joy" is mentioned over two hundred times in the Bible and "rejoice" over two hundred times. God's Word states that we should "Rejoice always" (1 Thessalonians 5:16) not be joyful when we have earned it.

There is even more danger from the reward illusion than robbing us of the joy God has designed for us. If we view God as someone we seek to be fair to, then we distort who God is and what he wants from us. This distortion leads us to think God cares more for our actions than for our acceptance, love and dependence. Then, when we compare his incredible love to our actions, the shame we feel from our failures even suggests His grace was not good enough. Like the control illusion, unless we strive to reject the reward illusion, we run the risk of losing hope and falling into apathy. As Augustine says "God has willed that our struggle should be with prayers rather than with our own strength."[5]

Another serious problem the reward illusion creates is we expect God to also be fair on our terms and within our understanding of the situation. Then, we lose faith when we see or contemplate suffering. This is especially common when the suffering hits us directly. There is no easy answer to this problem because the reward illusion is so strong. We must simply accept that there is more to God's plan than we can possibly know.

The drive for fairness is so powerful that it is even an instinct among dogs. A group of dogs was brought into a room and told to sit along a wall. Each dog was asked, in turn, to shake hands (paw) and received praise and a pat on the head for successfully completing the simple task. The dogs were then sent to sit along the opposite wall while a second group of dogs were brought in. The second group received a food treat for shaking hands while the first group watched. After witnessing this "unfair" treatment, the first group was no longer willing to shake hands for a simple pat on the head.[6]

Summary

"If anyone loves the world, love for the Father is not in them" (1 John 2:15). Remember from Chapter 1 that the meaning of love in this verse is what you want for yourself. If your identity is of a person seeking pleasure, a person who feels their conscious mind is in control and/or a person who seeks to be God's benefactor by paying Him back, then you have identified with the world. Scripture tells us to identify instead as a child of God created in His image.

We will never completely eliminate the three illusions. The selfish illusion which misunderstands what brings pleasure, the control illusion which misunderstands how our minds work and the reward illusion with misunderstands what God wants from us each can destroy our lives. And they are all driven through the heart so they continue to affect us even after we have a rational understanding of them. Constant vigilance can limit the harm they cause.

So now, let's look at what Scripture tells us and is confirmed by science on how to live in the image of God.

Part 2
LIVING IN THE IMAGE OF GOD

CHAPTER FIVE

A LIFE OF SUCCESS

"For I know the plans I have for you," declares the LORD,
"plans to prosper you and not to harm you, plans to give you
hope and a future"
(Jeremiah 29:11).

L iving in the image of our Creator means we are designed to create our accomplishments. Jesus said that if we follow Him, we will "receive many times as much in this age, and in the age to come, eternal life" (Luke 18:30), but the typical interpretation of the Bible calls on us to sacrifice in this life for those eternal rewards. The Bible can't teach both a better and a worse lifestyle, so let's examine which is correct.

It is difficult to come up with an interpretation of the words of Jesus that does not conclude that we are called to a better lifestyle. And why would God design anything else for His children? Accepting this interpretation sounds selfish, but it is what Jesus clearly said. Sometimes we may choose meaningful that pays less than we might receive in another job, but it is hardly a sacrifice to choose a path that brings better health and more happiness. However, you may be tricked into thinking it is a sacrifice if you fall for the selfish illusion and think you can gain more happiness through hedonistic pursuits.

So ask big of a big God. Look at the spectacular things God has done through so many people of lowly status. Dream big and do not let the false view of humility hold you back. The life God offers will bring more meaning and accomplishment than any alternative. And in the words of C.S. Lewis, you will be "surprised by joy."

So now let's look at the Christian advantage in the secular world, a redefinition of what Christianity should be about rather than those limiting concepts often associated with the Christian lifestyle and how to achieve this lifestyle through a purpose driven life. Then in future chapters, we will examine the health and happiness advantages of following Jesus.

Success in the Secular World

"Take delight in the Lord, and He will give you the desires of your heart" (Psalm 37:4). Since the middle ages, virtually all major inventions and scientific developments have come from Christian nations. Over this time, the economies of Christian nations have dramatically outpaced non-Christian ones. Today, the Chinese are seeing a more robust economy in areas where there is a significant number of Christians. Areas without Christians fail to keep up even if they have other religions.[1] Unfortunately, we see Christianity fading in Europe and North America. At the same time, we see the dominance in financial matters and intellectual discoveries in Europe and North America disappearing. This fact should not be dismissed as a simple coincidence.

The clear advantage from Christianity that this economic data shows is counter-intuitive with how business appears to operate. Unethical behavior appears to work, at least in the short term. Of course, sometimes ethical businesses fail and unethical ones are financially successful, so there are other factors at play beyond the Christian advantage. Let's explore why the teachings of Jesus helps us towards secular success.

The Power of Prayer

God answers prayer and guides us towards success. We do not see the overall picture, so sometimes it appears that praying for a situation did not work out. God answers prayer like a loving parent. Just as a parent knows not all requests are best for their child, so God, in His wisdom, does not always grant our petitions. And sometimes answers are delayed to encourage us to pray more, work harder or learn patience. God knows what is best for us and His role in our lives is a huge benefit.

Less Distraction from the Selfish Illusion

We are all distracted be the selfish illusion that deceitfully tells us we will get more pleasure from pursuing secular delights. We will never completely eliminate this powerful tool of Satan, but if we follow Jesus, we will be less distracted than those without the Christian benefit.

The Power of Humility

As we saw in Chapter 3, companies which embody a proper understanding of humility have a significant advantage. Much more is accomplished when employees are working for the company rather than for personal recognition, when employees have an open mind to learn and when employees seek to serve each other. These are the three aspects of humility in the image of God.

Public Relations

Companies who operate unethically court a public relations disaster. A positive reputation is a key for people wanting to do business with a company. The importance of a company's reputation is why so many companies contribute to charities. In the same way, your personal reputation is critical to your success if life.

Employee Productivity

Employees are easily distracted when they see unethical behavior. Further, seeing unethical actions increases the chances that they will also engage in inappropriate behavior to the detriment of the company.

Employee Recruitment and Retention

It is expensive to hire and train a good employee and important work can be missed when there is nobody in the job. A good reputation helps attract top employees. And once an employee is hired, unethical behavior leaves them less committed to the company. For employees, being recognized as ethical enhances promotions and job security.

Investment Opportunities

Investors look at the ethical reputation of a company and its leaders because they want to be comfortable that what is being presented is true. They also recognize the potential problems and scandals that can occur from unethical behavior.

Redefine Christianity

It is easy although not accurate to conclude that we are called to a restrictive life in the areas of dealing with oppression, financial management and appearance when we look at verses such as: "Turn to them the other cheek" (Matthew 5:39), "Sell your possessions and give to the poor" (Luke 12:33) and "People look at the outward appearance, but the Lord looks at the heart" (1 Samuel 16:7). Let's take a deeper look at what the Bible is really teaching.

Response to Oppression

Christian teachers have turned an important teaching from Jesus regarding turning the other cheek from passive resistance into passive acceptance. Looking at the context around what Jesus said paints the correct picture.

"Nazareth! Can anything good come from there?" (John 1:46). This verse has been interpreted to mean that Nazareth was a small, obscure town, but recent archeological science has determined that Nazareth was the site of a Roman garrison. This explains why Joseph would go there to find work as a carpenter. It means that Jesus grew up in a town that was under heavy Roman oppression.

The people Jesus preached to were primarily the oppressed, not the Pharisees that He criticized. So the crowd would see him as someone who understood the life of oppression and the limited choices the oppressed had in that society. They understood His "turn the other cheek" teaching as an act of defiance, but this meaning has been lost on us today.

Without understanding the context, the verse teaching "turn the other cheek" looks quite passive. "Do not resist an evil person. If anyone slaps you on the right cheek, turn to them the other cheek also" (Matthew 5:39). A slap on the right cheek is a backhand slap. It would have been something done in distain by a person who considered themselves superior to the person being slapped. The slap was a put-down more than an attempt to hurt.

Turning the other cheek was a provocative action that called for the oppressor to hit like an equal. Custom would not permit using the left hand to strike another backhanded slap because the left hand was considered unclean. So the brilliant solution Jesus offers puts the aggressor in an awkward position, not wanting to recognize the oppressed as an equal.

The teaching continues with "If anyone wants to sue you and take your shirt, hand over your coat as well" (Matthew 5:40). Here the translators use the misleading word "shirt" when translating the Greek word "chiton." It is misleading because shirts and pants were not worn at that time. Both men and women wore tunics, no underwear and a coat if necessary for warmth. So Jesus is saying go completely naked and thereby shame the person taking your tunic.

The third example Jesus gives to stand up against oppression follows when He said "If anyone forces you to go one mile, go with them two miles" (Matthew 5:41). The Romans had a form of postal system with posts set up a mile apart. Under the hated Roman law of Angaria, a Roman could demand that an inhabitant of an occupied territory carry messages or equipment to the next post. However, if someone is carrying for two miles, then the Roman could face disciplinary action for apparently demanding more that the law permitted.

The point of this teaching is that we are called to stand up for ourselves when faced with injustice, even when our options are limited. Passive resistance is not always an effective option, but it should be our first consideration. It certainly worked for Gandhi, who though not a Christian was inspired by Jesus.

Jesus follows this teaching by telling us to "love your enemies and pray for those who persecute you" (Matthew 5:44). We are to refrain from acting out of anger or revenge. Acting out of love means we do what we can to discourage oppressive actions for the benefit of the bully as well as for everyone who may be oppressed. In contrast, the passive acceptance that is generally taught can serve to encourage more bad behavior.

Financial Management

A frequently misunderstood passage in Scripture is where Jesus instructed the rich man to sell everything and give the money to the poor (Matthew 19:16-30). This was a situation where a rich man wanted to earn his way into heaven. The passage specifically speaks about salvation and Jesus made it quite clear that we can't earn our salvation.

When we are wealthy, we feel that we simply buy whatever we need. This is why Jesus said that "it is easier for a camel to go through the eye of a needle than for someone who is rich to enter the kingdom of God" (Matthew 19:24). In a way, wealth is a burden because when our material possessions become important to us, it is more difficult to fully accept Jesus. However, Jesus followed up on the discussion on salvation by saying "with man this is impossible, but with God all things are possible" (Matthew 19:26).

"Anyone who does not provide for their relatives, and especially for their own household, has denied the faith and is worse than an unbeliever" (1 Timothy 5:8). This verse shows the need for proper financial planning. Our planning should include resources set aside for contingencies as well as for meeting God's plan for your life. The purchases you require may be quite different from someone else, so don't compare yourself to others.

"Each of you should give what you have decided in your heart to give, not reluctantly or under compulsion, for the Lord loves a cheerful giver" (2 Corinthians 9:7). This verse covers any kind of support we offer, not just monetary giving. And in it, Paul is saying that pushing yourself to give is not the answer. Science confirms that we generally feel good when helping others and this brings us many health benefits. But when this was done out of a sense of obligation, the helpers felt disgust, contempt, stress and resentment towards those that they helped.[2]

Personal Appearance

"In everything set them a good example, doing what is good" (Titus 2:7). The fruits of the Holy Spirit, "love, joy, peace" (Galatians 5:22), are tremendous assets in helping others to accept Jesus. When they see such value radiating out of a Christian, they want the same for themselves. It is far better to maintain an appearance that will draw people in rather than practicing a misunderstanding of humility. Of course, you have to be careful that you idolize Jesus Christ rather than your personal appearance.

Ruth Graham believed that maintaining an attractive appearance was part of pleasing God. Shortly after they were married, they were travelling on a Crusade to Britain. Billy declined to wear his bright ties in deference to the conservative British custom. He said to Ruth, "In England, I guess you won't want to wear lipstick as you do at home. Church people over there might not understand." Ruth simply replied, "Don't you think that may be something on which the Lord expects us to help their understanding."[3] Look at what has happened with the quick fall of Christianity in Europe. Perhaps adopting an unattractive lifestyle had something to do with turning people away from Jesus.

The Purpose of Your Life

Life is much better when it is driven by the purpose God has set out for you. This purpose simplifies your life with meaningful goals. Yet, even knowing your purpose is not enough. It is also vital to embrace it in your heart. Sadly, most people drift without seeking to understand their purpose.

There is no single lifestyle appropriate for all Christians. Your purpose in life should define your lifestyle rather than seeking to adapt a purpose for the lifestyle you seek to enjoy. The selfish illusion demonstrates that we will not have a net increase in our happiness through materialism or hedonism, but like the other two spiritual illusions, it is hard to combat. A clear purpose is a strong weapon against Satan's deception contained in the selfish illusion.

It starts with God

Life without God is meaningless. Fortunately, basic metaphysics shows us there is a God. The world must have been created by some superior being as the universe is simply too unstable to otherwise exist through the infinity of time. The fact that religion has often abused the concept of God does not in any way negate His existence.

Once we accept that God exists, by faith, reason or both, living our lives with the concept of eternity puts things in an entirely different perspective. Our lives are both a test and a trust in being good servants of the talents God has given to us. "For we are God's handiwork, created in Christ Jesus to do good works, which God prepared in advance for us to do" (Ephesians 2:10).

Accept and relate to God

Finding and deeply embracing the purpose God has for you requires that you accept Jesus as your personal savior. After you accept Jesus, you can enter into a personal relationship with Him. All relationships have their ups and downs, so you should be prepared for that.

In the words of Craig Groeschal, "If prayer isn't necessary to accomplish your plans, you aren't thinking big enough." So "Pray continually" (1 Thessalonians 5:17). Some Christians question if it is possible to be continually in prayer. If we are consistently seeking to identify with God in His image, then we are in a type of prayer.

Close spiritual encounters with God feel wonderful and can change your life. We are all created in the image of God and commanded to identify with Him, but we are different in the ways that work best for us in relating to Him. Gary Thomas explored the different ways in which Christians find intimacy with God in his book Sacred Pathways. Focus on those ways that work best for you.

- Naturalists relate to the beauty of God's creation outdoors.
- Sensates relate to worship that involves sight, sound, smell, taste and touch.
- Traditionalists relate through liturgies and symbols that don't change over time.
- Ascetics relate through solitude and simplicity.
- Activists relate through battling evil and working for a better world.
- Caregivers relate through caring for those in need.
- Enthusiasts relate through celebration.

- Contemplatives relate through adoration.
- Intellectuals relate through study.4

Your purpose is significant

You are acting in the image of God. Reflect on the awesome potential that this brings as you work in line with God. You have been given certain talents, so use them where they will be effective.

It is not just about you

Many young people today say they are spiritual but not religious. This usually means that they sense something greater than themselves. Their spiritual moments tend to be personal experiences that they are reluctant to share. Typically, they resist a personal relationship with Jesus because they see so many abuses by people claiming to be Christians. Of course, there are problems within every Christian denomination since people make mistakes, but these are our mistakes, not God's.

The Christian spiritual encounters are stronger than non-believers experience because we have a personal relationship with Jesus. "Like newborn babies, crave pure spiritual milk" (1 Peter 2:2). But we can fall into a trap with making our lives just about these experiences. We are called to both experience God and to fulfill His purpose for our lives.

Listen to God

Not long ago, I heard a story about a young man and an old preacher. The young man lost his job and didn't know which way to turn. So he went to see the old preacher.

Pacing about the preacher's study, the young man ranted about his problem. Finally, he clenched his fist and shouted, "I've begged God to say something to help me, preacher, why doesn't God answer?"

The old preacher, who sat across the room, spoke something in reply, something so hushed it was indistinguishable. The young man stepped across the room. "What did you say?" he asked. The preacher repeated himself, but again in a tone as soft as a whisper. So the young man moved closer until he was leaning on the preacher's chair.

"Sorry," he said. "I still didn't hear you." With their heads bent together, the old preacher spoke once more. "God sometimes whispers," he said, "so we will move closer to him." This time, the young man heard and he understood.

We all want God's voice to thunder through the air with the answer to our problem. But God's is the still, small voice...the gentle whisper. Perhaps there's a reason.

Nothing draws human focus quite like a whisper. God's whisper means I must stop my ranting and move close to Him, until my head is bent together with His. And then, as I listen, I will find my answer.

Better still, I find myself closer to God. And there is no better place to be.

- Author unknown

Look at your motive

Our motive should be based on the greatest commandment which involves all our heart, soul and mind. If we are able to reach an identity is based around life in His image, then our motives will be pure. We will never reach the perfection of the "all" called for in the greatest commandment, but growth in that direction is a primary part of our purpose on earth.

The reward illusion teaches us that nothing we do is going to make God love us more. Our purpose should not be based on feeble efforts to repay God but rather one that seeks to live through His purpose for us. Our actions based around living in the image of God help to transform us.

Purpose that is consistent, clear and comfortable

You will find a variety of purposes in your life when you consider various elements such as family, career, friends, neighborhood and interests. Many of these will change over time. God's purpose for you may be obvious or it may take effort to understand. Perhaps it will require you to experiment in some areas. Embrace life with a purpose that is consistent, clear and comfortable.

Consistent means it is in line with the greatest commandment to love God. Drawing on the work of Augustine, we have determined this means to identify with the image of God. This leads to actions that obtain the basic needs to accomplish His purpose for us, thinking clearly along the lines taught by Jesus and loving through the inspiration of the Holy Spirit. This contrasts with secular goals such as pleasure, power, fame and fortune.

Unless the purpose is clear, we will fall into the trap of being too busy to accomplish what is most important. Further, a clear purpose allows us to analyze what are the basic needs to accomplish that purpose.

Finally, your purpose needs to be something you want to accomplish both in your conscious mind and your heart. What others might see as a sacrifice, we do simply because that is what we love to do. Look at how Augustine taught about love: "it makes easy whatever is difficult, it gives newness to what has become a habit and it gives irresistible force to the movement toward the supreme God."[5]

Summary

It is time to set aside the notion that Christians are called to a life of sacrifice. The only thing we are called to give up are those illusions that will not increase our happiness. So let's re-define Christianity to become a life that others will want when they see it. The evidence shows that Christianity brings greater success in the secular world. Later in this book, we will explore how Christianity also delivers greater health and happiness.

God the Father has created us for a purpose. By living according to this purpose, in turn we create things through our accomplishments. Of course, we are much more than our secular success. Let us now explore how our minds are designed to function in the image of God.

CHAPTER SIX

THINK LIKE JESUS

"Jesus answered: 'I am the way, the truth and the life'"
(John 14:6).

T he control illusion, which teaches that our thoughts are dominated by what happens in our unconscious minds, presents a difficult conundrum for non-believers. It makes them feel as if they are driven by desires beyond their control. Or they simply ignore it and live their lives trying to forget about this uncomfortable situation. In contrast, Christians can take comfort that our lives are guided by the Holy Spirit.

"Aristotle thought that all human action was to achieve happiness. Nietzsche thought that all human action was to get power. Freud thought that all human action was to avoid anxiety."[1] All these ideas have some merit but are ultimately flawed. Jesus gave us the truth.

Freud started the ball rolling regarding the importance of the unconscious mind. We have used the word heart because that is the word used in Biblical translations. Feelings are thoughts coming from the heart that our conscious minds can recognize, but we do not even feel most of our unconscious thoughts. In the words of Timothy Wilson: "According to the modern perspective, Freud's view of the unconscious was far too limited. When he said that consciousness was the tip of the mental iceberg, he was short of the mark by quite a bit—it may be more the size of the snowball on top of the iceberg".[2] Our conscious minds sometimes get distracted by several thoughts at the same time, but that is nothing compared to the number of thoughts the heart is generating.

Esteemed scientist Mihaly Csikszentmihalyi said: "Contrary to what we tend to assume, the normal state of the mind is chaos...when we are left alone, with no demands on attention, the basic order of the mind reveals itself...Entropy is the normal state of consciousness—a condition that is neither useful nor enjoyable".[3] This uncomfortable feeling is why is why Freud felt all human action was directed to relieving this discomfort. A series of 11 studies found that participants typically did not enjoy spending 6 to 15 minutes alone with nothing to do but think. Many even chose to give themselves electric shocks to break up the discomfort of their mind left alone to think.[4] With so many thoughts racing through our bodies at once, you can understand why thinking clearly is a priority the mind tries to achieve.

Obviously, we want our minds to function with the love, joy and peace that are the fruits of the Holy Spirit (Galatians 5:12), so let's explore how we can mature in that direction.

It Starts with Accepting Jesus

"If anyone is in Christ, the new creation has come" (2 Corinthians 5:17). Accepting Jesus is more than a get out of hell free card. If we are open to fully accepting Him, then there is an incredible change in how our heart behaves. We may not fully appreciate what the Holy Spirit is doing because it is through our heart, but we are in a much better place than non-believers. The more deeply we accept Jesus, the greater the benefits we receive.

At first, the idea of surrendering your life to Jesus sounds like a difficult teaching. Why would anyone want to give up their life? Yet, when we look at it another way, surrendering to Jesus becomes the obvious choice. Our minds are created in the image of God and Jesus teaches us about the way our minds were intended to think. So surrendering to Jesus is like using our minds the way the "owner's manual" says to use them. If we employ our minds in any other way, it is like mixing diesel fuel with the gasoline in our car.

C.S. Lewis used this car analogy when he wrote: "God made us, or invented us, as a man invents an engine. A car is made to run on gasoline and it would not run properly on anything else. Now God designed the human machine to run on Himself. He, Himself, is the fuel our spirits were designed to burn. He is the food our spirits were designed to feed on. There is no other. That is why is it just no good asking God to make us happy without Himself. God cannot give us happiness and peace apart from Himself because it is not there. There is no such thing."[5]

Surrender implies a life of sacrifice where we submit to being passive slaves to God. The reality is that we retain our free will, our personal preferences and our use of analytical thinking. We are to take on an active role in gaining understanding, inspiring others and achieving accomplishments.

We are called to use our minds in the way they were designed in the image of God. Listen to God in your heart, knowing that He plans for you to live a life that is more productive, happier and more full of love than any other path you could choose.

The Bible Brings Understanding

"Like newborn babies, crave pure spiritual milk, so that by it you may grow up in your salvation, now that you have tasted that the Lord is good" (1 Peter 2:2-3). Atheists are quick to abuse the Bible because they don't understand it. When we truly seek understanding, then we crave for more and God delivers.

The Bible is not just another book. Augustine said: "The wisdom of what a person says is in direct proportion to his progress in learning the Holy Scriptures – and I am not speaking of intensive reading or memorization, but real understanding and careful investigation of their meaning. Some people read them but neglect them: by their reading they profit in knowledge, by their neglect they forfeit understanding."[6] This quote contains two important messages.

The first message is that without the teachings of the Bible, a person can't develop wisdom. This is a stronger statement about the importance of the Bible than we typically hear, even among devout Christians. It would not be considered politically appropriate today.

The second message is that intensive reading and memorization is not enough. He calls for careful investigation, which means seeking other sources to explain what the Bible is teaching. If we don't do so, then we "forfeit understanding." Simple reading is much easier than careful investigation, but if we love God in the sense of wanting to be like him, we will willingly make the effort.

The careful investigation of the Bible that Augustine calls for involves outside sources as well as using verses within it to help us understand other verses. For example, in Chapter 1, we used other verses to interpret the meaning of love in the greatest commandment. Yet, this is not always enough. Much of the Book of Revelations makes no sense without understanding the context.

Why did God make the Bible so complex? Augustine says "some of the expressions are so obscure as to shroud the meaning in the thickest darkness. And I do not doubt that all this was divinely arranged for the purpose of subduing pride by toil, and of preventing a feeling of satiety in the intellect, which generally holds in small esteem what is discovered without difficulty."[7]

Despite this complexity, the Bible is of great value for everyone to read and study. Augustine taught that "the Bible was composed in such a way that as beginners mature, its meaning grows with them."[8] God's truth is revealed through Scripture at many different levels. The deeper you investigate, the more you realize how much more there is to learn. Investigation brings both greater appreciation and a deeper love for Bible study. "It is the glory of God to conceal a matter; to search out a matter is the glory of kings" (Proverbs 25:2).

An open mind is key to understanding the Bible. It is human nature to be reluctant to change our interpretation of a given passage once we have been taught what it means. Yet, Christian pastors differ greatly in the many interpretations that they teach. They can't all be right and we have to be careful that they don't lead us astray despite their best intentions.

Augustine addressed the importance of keeping an open mind when he wrote: "In matters that are obscure and far beyond our vision, even in such as we may find treated in Holy Scripture, different interpretations are sometimes possible without prejudice to the faith we have received. In such a case we should not rush in headlong and so firmly take our stand on one side that, if further progress in the search of truth justly undermines this position, we too fall with it."[9]

Unfortunately, we see Christians abandon their faith rather than recognize that they may have an incorrect interpretation of Scripture. Others may downgrade the importance of the Bible in their daily lives because they are uncomfortable with the teachings. Neither approach is the appropriate way to treat the Word of God.

Augustine quotes the apostle Paul in teaching that the Bible uses illustrations that should not be taken literally. He writes: "At the outset, you must be very careful lest you take figurative expressions literally. What the apostle says pertains to this problem: 'for the letter kills, but the spirit gives life.'"[10] Augustine interprets this verse found in 2 Corinthians 3:6 to mean that we must focus on the meaning behind the message rather than the literal words used because insisting on a literal interpretation can sometimes get us into trouble. Yet a focus on a literal interpretation is a strong trend among many Christians today.

There are some verses in the Bible that are obviously not intended for literal translation. Virtually all Christians feel the verses where trees (Isaiah 55:12) and rivers (Psalm 98:8) clap their hands are allegorical. And having a "plank in your own eye" (Matthew 7:3) is obviously an exaggeration. Part of the complexity of the Bible is our not knowing exactly where to draw the line with respect to a literal interpretation.

God can do anything including giving hands to the trees, but we want to know what He did do rather than what He can do. The point Augustine makes is that sometimes it is impossible for us to know if a given passage is allegorical. Let's turn to Scripture to be our guide in dealing with this issue. Scripture tells us the gospel of Luke is historically accurate because it says "I too decided to write an orderly account for you, most excellent Theophilus, so that you know the certainty of the things you have been taught" (Luke 1:3-4). Of course, it matters that the words, death and resurrection of Jesus are historically accurate.

For the rest of the Bible, let's concentrate on the message God has sent us. It should not matter to our faith how long the days were during the creation of the earth. Augustine said "what kind of days these were is extremely difficult, or perhaps impossible for us to conceive."[11] Augustine emphasizes the point of concentrating on what matters when he wrote "The Spirit of God, who was speaking through them [the Biblical authors], did not wish to teach people about such things that would contribute nothing to their salvation.[12]

Recognize that the Bible is in great disrepute in the secular world and avoid falling into these traps. Atheists will look at a specific interpretation of Scripture and say the whole Bible is inaccurate rather than accepting that their interpretation of that passage is wrong. Another problem is that many Christians treat the Bible as a rulebook. However, Jesus came to fulfill the law (Matthew 5:17) so that we are not bound to the 613 commandments of the Mosaic law. "The former regulation was set aside because it was weak and useless" (Hebrews 7:18).

"If you believe what you like in the gospels, and reject what you don't like, it is not the gospel you believe, but yourself." This quote is generally attributed to Augustine and speaks to the need to study the Bible and be prepared to change our understandings. When conflicts arise, it is time for a more detailed study of the verse in question. Proper study will enhance our faith rather than detract from it.

Sometimes when we read the Bible, we are like the Ethiopian eunuch and can't understand it "unless someone explains it to me" (Acts 8:31). This passage teaches that we should call on others to help us with difficult passages. Yet at the same time, we know that even our best experts come up with different interpretations. So we are called to our own reflections and to carefully listen to what God is saying to us. Augustine embraced everything he could to better understand Scripture including history, math, science, logic and the help of others while asking God to "open the ears of my heart". God's Word is important enough for us to do the same.

Worship in the Daily Christian Life

Worshipping God is vital to the Christian life. When Jesus taught us to pray through the Lord's Prayer, He started it with worship. However, just like we saw with humility, if we misunderstand what worship is about, then we will lose benefits. So, let's start with an exploration of the wrong reasons to worship.

As discussed in Chapter 1, the greatest commandment to love God is not a call for worship. The Reward Illusion leads us to think that we need to earn our favor with God and worship is the chosen way to do so. Effective worship requires us to look at a different purpose for worship, because God did not create us because He felt a desire for praise.

Worship is also not intended to put us in our place before God, which inevitably leads us to put ourselves above those who do not actively worship. This is the false humility we discussed in Chapter 3. We sometimes think of the Pharisee who thanked God that he was not like the tax collector (Luke 18:11) as only relevant to Biblical times, but these attitudes remain common today. Richard Beck, the Chair of Psychology at Abilene Christian University, writes with an admitted exaggeration about how Christians tip and behave at lunch after Sunday service. "If you have ever worked in the restaurant industry, you know the reputation of the Sunday morning lunch crowd...Never has a more well-dressed, entitled, dismissive, haughty or cheap collection of Christians been seen on the face of the earth."[13]

Six significant reasons exist to make worship a central part of our lives, replacing the incorrect reasons of earning favor with God and false humility. These are:

We tend to do what our heart focuses on

As we saw in Chapter 2, if we set our identity as in the image of God and consistently reinforce what God is, then we will tend to act accordingly. The control illusion lets us think that our intellect is in charge, but both Scripture and science teach us that it is an illusion. The greatest commandment is about a desire to become like God to the best of our abilities and worship helps us grow in that direction.

Worship brings joy

C.S. Lewis says "In commanding us to glorify Him, God is inviting us to enjoy Him."[14] The enjoyment of thinking about God and the anticipation of sharing eternity with Him is a special part of our love for God. Joyful worship also encourages our growth.

Worship brings self-confidence

Our attitude receives a tremendous boost when we remember throughout the day that God is with us. Norman Vincent Peale wrote *The Power of Positive Thinking* in 1952 and was recognized as the top motivational speaker of his generation. He writes:

> "One of the most powerful concepts, one which is a sure cure for lack of confidence, is the thought that God is actually with you and helping you. This is one of the simplest teachings in religion, namely, that the Almighty God will be your companion, will stand by you, help you, and see you through. No other idea is so powerful in developing self-confidence as this simple belief when practiced. To practice it simply affirm 'God is with me, God is helping me, God is guiding me.'"[15]

Gratitude brings personal benefits

As will be discussed in Chapter 7, expressing gratitude to others, including God, brings both physical and mental benefits to us.

Worship supports others

Christian worship involves both individual time with God and worship within groups. Since we are created for relationships, the group worship dynamic is important for encouraging each other. "Let us consider how we may spur one another on toward love and good deeds, not giving up meeting together as some are in the habit of doing" (Hebrews 10:24-25).

God responds to prayers

Jesus taught us to start our prayers with worship and we have evidence that God answers prayers. For example, skeptical medical historian Jacalyn Duffin of Queens University did a study of 1,400 documented medical miracles over the past 500 years. Her conclusion, based on overwhelming evidence, was that she believed in miracles.[16]

The Use and Limitations of Science

Clear thought is the second natural priority of the mind, so the systematic study should have a role in our life. Systematic study is the definition of science, but there is a gulf between Christianity and the scientific community. Many young people are lost because they feel a need to choose between competing systems. Science can and should be used to strengthen our Christian journey and be used to help bring non-believers to Jesus. It is far easier to accept and live the Biblical message when we see that science is backing it up. Thus, scientific understanding can become part of our practical faith.

Christians should take credit for science because the scientific method was developed in Christian nations. The scientific method is not found in ancient Greek or Chinese civilizations that are often most credited for the development of knowledge. Look at the words of one of our greatest astronomers, Johannes Kepler, "God, like a Master Builder, has laid the foundation of the world according to law and order. God wanted us to recognize those laws by creating us after His image so we could share in His own thought. Love the Lord your God with all your mind—and people did. The vast majority of the pioneers of science, William of Ockham, Francis Bacon, Galileo, Copernicus, Blaise Pascal, Joseph Priestley and Isaac Newton (who ended up writing commentaries on Revelation)—viewed their work as learning to think God's thoughts."[17]

Other famous scientists who expressed their belief in God include Louis Pasteur, Max Plank, Erwin Schrodinger, Thomas Edison, Guglielmo Marconi and Albert Einstein. Even atheist hero Charles Darwin said "I think the theory of evolution is fully compatible with faith in God. I think the greatest argument for the existence of

God is the impossibility of demonstrating and understanding that the immense universe, sublime above all measure, and man were the result of chance."

As valuable as science is to our understanding, it suffers from being incomplete. In the words of Pope Francis, "It cannot be maintained that empirical science provides a complete explanation of life, the interplay of all creatures and the whole of reality. This would be to breach the limits imposed by its own methodology."[18] A review of the methodology shows where things have gone wrong.

The scientific method provides an incomplete understanding because it is designed to exclude concepts that can't be confirmed. Under the scientific method, this confirmation is in the form of testing an element and seeing if it brings a different result from the same test with a control group where the element is not introduced. Anything with a supernatural component can't be tested in this way, meaning science can test God's creation but not God Himself.

Over the past century, scientists have used peer-reviewed journals to publicize their work. The peer-review process has so increased the rigor around the scientific method that now it is ingrained as a virtual requirement for information taught at university. This has even spilled over into the humanities as the peer review process seeks confirmation of the content found in academic journal articles. It is useful to engage in this systematic study as long as we recognize that the scientific method does not cover everything. The scientific community ignores this fact and thus leads many people away from God.

We must also be aware of bad science. Interpretations are sometimes made beyond what the data shows. And the scientist could be incompetent or dishonest. Surveys are often promoted as scientific, but they do not follow the scientific method with a control group. The result from a survey can be dramatically changed by the way the question is raised.

These limitations and problems around science provoke many Christians to simply ignore the appropriate role science in their daily lives. The scientific studies we see from Christian sources is typically seek to confirm the historical accuracy of their Biblical interpretation. We need much more scientific analysis regarding the message of the Bible rather than leaving it to the atheists to claim science and thereby lead people away from God.

Acting with a Clear Mind

Augustine taught that we are created in the image of Jesus in our ability to understand. This gives us the second natural priority of the mind, which is to think clearly. Two areas where we accomplish this is through establishing good habits and in reaching the state of flow.

Habits

"Do everything without grumbling or arguing" (Philippians 2:14). Our habits make it easier to accomplish those repetitive tasks without arguing with ourselves about when or if we will do them today. This frees the mind to think clearly and focus on what lies ahead. We often find our greatest inspiration during a mundane task such as taking a shower.

Scripture says to "train yourself to be godly" (1 Timothy 4:7). Training involves frequent repetition to develop abilities in whatever we are training for. Since the greatest commandment calls on us to develop ourselves in the image of God, it is natural that the Bible would call for us to develop such habits.

Christians who develop the habit of a set time each day to connect with God report incredible benefits. A time for prayer, a quiet time to listen to God and a time for Bible study are all habits too valuable to be excluded from daily life because we are too busy.

Finding Flow

Flow is a mental state where our mind is completely focused on the activity we are involved with in. It brings us to our highest level of effectiveness along with incredible enjoyment. Based on what we see in the Bible, Jesus was in the state of flow when He taught. After He gave the Sermon on the Mount, "the crowds were amazed at His teaching, because He taught as one who had authority, not as their teachers of the law" (Matthew 7: 28-29). In another example, "people were amazed" (Mark 1:22) when He taught at the synagogue.

Several experiences are associated with flow, although some are not always present. These are:

- A complete focus on the activity, like a deep involvement in a video game
- A feeling of serenity and loss of any self-consciousness, like an actor immersed within a role
- A feeling of personal control over the situation despite the challenges, like a chess grandmaster
- Great inner clarity, like a surgeon in a delicate operation
- A sense that time slows down, like an athlete "in the zone"
- A lack of awareness of physical needs, like the artist who forgets to eat.

To reach the state of flow, a clear, challenging and obtainable goal must be present. The person must have a high skill level and be intrinsically motivated to accomplish it. It is not an all or nothing sort of psychological state. And the energy level required takes a toll, so we can't remain in the state of flow indefinitely.

Our purpose in life should involve periods where we function in the state of flow. If your purpose never takes you to the state of flow, then you are not making full use of the talents God has given you.

Meditation, Distraction and Addiction

Other ways to quiet the mind exist besides engaging in habits or achieving the state of flow. These include meditation, distraction and chemical means. Thinking clearly is a natural priority of the mind, so we often go to great lengths to get our minds into a state where we are not bombarded by multiple thoughts at once. Remember the studies that we referenced earlier in this chapter where some people preferred electrical shocks to being alone with the discomfort of their chaotic mind.

Many different types of meditation are available to calm the mind. Eastern religions like Taoism teach that the quiet mind is the natural state and call for meditation to achieve this. While there is great value in Christian meditation when done as contemplative prayer, science shows that the Eastern religions are wrong as to the natural state of our minds.

Distraction can also serve to quiet the mind. Activities such as reading a novel or watching television can be effective. Exercise is especially effective as the mind focuses on the physical activity rather than on extraneous thoughts. Or, we can be so busy that we don't have time to think. Yet, with all of these options available, sometimes we are driven to do something more.

Chemicals such a drugs and alcohol are a fast and effective way to control the anxiety arising from an active mind. They are also dangerous, especially for those people who have a genetic predisposition to a certain chemical. While some chemicals can target pleasure centers in the brain, calming the mind is often the driving factor coming from the heart. Clear thinking means freedom from the uncomfortable chaos the mind finds in its natural state. A person high on drugs or alcohol may not be thinking rationally, but they feel as if they are thinking very clearly.

Christian Perfection

Jesus said, "Be perfect, therefore, as your heavenly Father is perfect" (Matthew 5:48). John Wesley, the pastor credited with founding the Methodist denomination, did not shy away from dealing with Christian perfection in a direct way. He said, "The word perfect is what many cannot bear. The very sound is an abomination to them...But are they not found in the oracles of God? If so, by what authority can any messenger of God lay them aside?"

The Christian perfection that Wesley taught was "humble, gentle, patient love for God and our neighbor ruling our tempers, words and actions." It is "purity of intention" and a "restoration to the image of God." He did not speak of "sinless perfection" because of the different understandings of what constitutes sin. A person achieving Christian perfection is still subject to temptations, errors in judgment, infirmities and a lack of knowledge.

Wesley taught that Christian perfection could be achieved in this life, usually many years after justification through accepting Jesus as Savior. Thus, he preached the need for continued growth. To back up his idea that Christian perfection is possible, he quoted Scripture verses, such as "love is made complete among us" (1 John 4:17). While the perfection Wesley preached may not be possible, it is good to seek a higher standard.[19]

The perfection teaching from Jesus is contrary to the call for moderation found in the golden mean of Aristotle, the middle way of Buddha, the doctrine of the mean from Confucius or the teachings of the Jewish scholar Maimonides. Mother Teresa said "I have found the paradox that if I love until it hurts, then there is no more hurt, only more love."

In our journey towards perfection in the image of God, it is important to distinguish between what science calls perfectionist strivings and perfectionist concerns. Perfectionist strivings are positive as long as they are not accompanied by perfectionist concerns. Unfortunately, the two are often seen together and this leads to psychological problems.

Michelangelo said "trifles make perfection and perfection is no trifle." Beyond great artists, we marvel at the skill of athletes honed through years of intense training. And if you are going into heart surgery, you certainly hope the surgeon has sought perfection in developing his or her craft. Clearly a place exists for perfectionist strivings.

Of course, we don't reach absolute perfection and sometime fall far short. Perfectionist concerns arise when a person feels constant pressure to achieve their ideal. A life with perfectionist concerns exhibits problems both along the way and at the time of the eventual failure. These concerns can lead to depression, suicide, seeking sympathy, substance abuse, procrastination, anxiety, heart problems, narcissism and social alienation.

Problems also surface when perfectionist tendencies are out of balance with the task to be performed. In the workplace, this results in low productivity and workaholism. Workaholics are sometimes praised for their dedication, but it is a serious societal problem.

Another trap in our striving for perfection is what scientists call moral licensing. This is the tendency to engage in bad behavior but justify it to ourselves based on our past good behavior. Jesus illustrated this in the parable of the good Samaritan (Luke 10:30-37). A priest and later a Levite passed the man in need without offering any help. The priest and the Levite would have been recognized as men of God and the Samaritan as an outsider in the Jewish culture. To avoid the trap of moral licensing, we can adopt the attitude that our past good deeds have trained us to do more rather than less. Jesus said "By this everyone will know that you are my disciples, if you love one another" (John 13:35). Rather than judging yourself worthy of bad behavior, continually ask yourself why you are seeking perfection in the image of God and focus on values.

So how do we strive for perfection in our love of God while minimizing the perfectionist concern that we will never measure up? The keys are humility and joy. When we accept humility in the manner discussed in Chapter 3, we can strive towards perfection in our image of God without feeling the pressure to accomplish it. We are on earth to enjoy our walk with the Lord, not to worry about our performance.

Summary

Having multiple thoughts going through our minds at the same time is not comfortable. Chaos reigns deep within the minds of most people and displays itself in the form of anxiety. We control it through focusing on whatever lies in front of us, thereby seeking to think clearly. This is a coping strategy that does not really solve the problem. Most of our thoughts are coming from the heart that we can't control.

The solution starts with a deep acceptance of Jesus. This leads us to crave God's Word and to spend time worshiping Him. Our anxiety can then be replaced with the first fruits of the Holy Spirit, love, joy and peace.

So in giving us the greatest commandment, God has instructed us to strive for a different and better standard than Christians are typically taught. By accepting and then craving to live our identity in His image, we are able to love God in our hearts. This leads to radiance we sometimes see in Christians that draws others to the faith. It is not easy and we will sometimes fall back, but that is what thinking like Jesus is all about. Imagine the radiance He brought into a room.

CHAPTER SEVEN

THE FIRE OF THE
HOLY SPIRIT

*"For we are God's handiwork,
created in Christ Jesus to do good works"*
(Ephesians 2:10).

Helping others is the third natural priority of the human mind, but it is not just any sort of helping. We generally value a gift by what it costs. This way of thinking is limiting because it is the gift of your spirit that truly connects with other people. Science shows that we receive health benefits from altruistic behavior. Altruistic behavior is not occasional good deeds. Christians are to "devote themselves to doing what is good" (Titus 3:8). The word "devote" shows that we need the love mindset all the time. This devotion towards helping others throughout the day is how we seek to be like God and thereby follow His greatest commandment.

Jesus taught "Do to others as you would have them do to you" (Luke 6:31). Christians typically take this to mean not to do bad things to other people, but if Jesus meant that to be the focus, then He would have given us a "don't do" teaching. He knew that we receive benefits in this life from altruism because we are created in His image.

A gift can meet a physical need such as giving money to buy food, an intellectual need such as teaching a skill to someone or an emotional need such as making another person feel that they are valuable. Both physical and intellectual gifts are important as we have seen since meeting basic needs and thinking clearly are the first and second priorities of the mind. Yet, it is the emotional gifts that we, as Christians, should always be on the lookout to give. Sometimes an emotional gift can be easy to give such as a simple word of encouragement.

As we will explore in this chapter, we receive many health benefits when we help others, but this is not always the case. Science shows that to receive these benefits, we should be non-judgmental, focused on the present and not be giving out of a sense of obligation.[1] So again, we see science demonstrating the truth of the Bible. "Each of you should give what you have decided in your heart to give, not reluctantly or under compulsion, for the Lord loves a cheerful giver" (2 Corinthians 9:7).

Born to Be Good

We are created in the image of God, yet the secular world has a hard time accepting that this means a loving nature. Niccolo Machiavelli wrote "Men never do good unless necessity drives them to it."[2] Science shows that Machiavelli is simply wrong.[3,4,5] We have both a loving nature and a tendency to sin because the selfish illusion makes us think it will increase our pleasure.

We are created with a basic desire within our hearts to love others. As a child learns selfishness, this loving nature is weakened, but it does not totally disappear. In the words of Dacher Keltner of the University of California at Berkley, "It has long been assumed that selfishness, greed and competitiveness lie at the core of human behavior...But clearly, recent scientific findings forcefully challenge this view of human nature. We see that compassion is deeply rooted in our brains."[6] With the grace of the Holy Spirit, our hearts can be renewed to their loving nature and our lives will be healthier and happier.

Our review of infant behavior starts with twins in the womb. At fourteen weeks after conception, twins will reach towards each other. By eighteen weeks, 30% of their movement is the deliberate stroking of the head or back of the other twin.[7] Clearly, the babies do not have the brain development to reason that they will get nice strokes in return for giving them. Rather their desire to be kind is natural.

A newborn will cry in support of another baby. It is common in a nursery for the cry of one infant to set off a chain reaction. A baby will also cry when listening to a recording of another baby crying. However, the baby will not respond to a recording of its own cry.[8]

A baby is able to make complex social judgments at six months. A study at Yale University tested babies using a puppet show. A puppet tried to get up a toy mountain while the babies watched. Then another puppet was introduced to help the first puppet scale the mountain by pushing him from behind. Finally, a third puppet was introduced that knocked the climbing puppet back to the foot of the mountain. After the scene was replayed several times, the babies were given the chance to play with either the helper puppet or the hindering puppet. They overwhelmingly chose the helper puppet.[9]

By twelve months, babies seek to be active helpers. They will comfort someone in distress or point to something that apparently has been lost.[10] An eighteen-month toddler will pick up a clothespin or open a door for an unrelated adult to be helpful.[11]

Another study of eighteen-month toddlers found that they exhibited greater happiness in giving treats than in getting treats. And they found the greatest happiness when the toddlers were giving from their own resources so that they would have less for themselves.[12]

It is often assumed that a baby is born to be selfish because of the negative behavior observed when a toddler learns to say "no". Consider other alternatives to this action before we assume a natural inclination to power and selfishness instead of love. Children learn from mimicry and the toddler would have been told "no" countless time by its parents. Another explanation is that children crave attention and saying "no" gets attention from adults.

A study at Harvard with three-year-olds showed the children had a natural inclination to share. A prize was contained in back of a long, transparent box while two children were left alone in an observation room. The box had a rope on each side so that if the children co-operated and each pulled on the rope, the prize (such as gummy bears) would come out through a hole in the box. In more than 70% of the cases, the child who got the reward first shared it equally with the other child. The children rarely argued and virtually no physical conflict occurred.[13]

The obvious question in light of scientific findings like these is why we witness so many situations of bad behavior from young children. Unless there is a good explanation for the bad behavior we observe, it is difficult to accept that we are created with the natural inclination to love and help others. The explanation for selfish behaviors comes from the slow development of specific brain regions and from the unintended consequences of what we teach our children.

A brain area that lags in development is the right temporal-parietal junction (RTPJ). The RTPJ is a part of the brain involved in understanding a situation from another person's point of view.[14] The child may not realize what is obvious to us. We assume that all areas of the brain develop along an equal path, but that is not reality. Certain aspects of social intelligence will be well developed in a child while other aspects take more time. In some situations, a child may simply not understand what the other child is thinking rather than not having a naturally loving nature.

The other reason we see bad behavior in children is that they have been conditioned to act that way from mimicking their caregivers. Think about the many times an object of interest to a baby is snatched away. While removing the object may be done for the baby's own good, nevertheless the baby learns to snatch away objects. When a toddler snatches something, it is mimicking a learned behavior rather than acting the way its mind was created.

In the same way, when a toddler learns to say no, it is mimicking behavior. As well, it gets attention which it loves. So we should not be quick to assume that what we observe around a toddler learning the word "no" means there is an innate desire for power.

Total Depravity

Total depravity is a doctrine about human nature that is found in the statement of faith of some churches and has different interpretations among clergy. To some, it means we need grace from God before we can effectively relate to Him. To others, it involves how we relate to God but also includes the idea that people are totally selfish when they interact with each other, except for those who have accepted Jesus and then God works through them.

Logic indicates we should reject the second interpretation of total depravity that defines human nature as totally selfish. C.S. Lewis writes: "I disbelieve the doctrine, partly on the logical grounds that if our depravity were total we should not know ourselves to be depraved, and partly because experience shows us much goodness in human nature."[15] We have seen in Chapter 2 the powerful effect of the identity you adopt, so it is important to accept that we are created to be good in the image of the God.

A Gift of the Heart

"A generous person will prosper; whoever refreshes others will be refreshed" (Proverbs 11:25).

Maturing in the image of the Holy Spirit means developing compassion. According to definitions typically used by scientists who study giving, compassion is the desire to give where there is a concern for the welfare of the recipient. Empathy is feeling what the other person feels and sympathy is a concern about their problem, but these do not necessarily invoke a desire to act. Pity is bad because it includes a condescending attitude.

There are so many scientific studies demonstrating the health and happiness benefits of acting compassionately, that if we understand these benefits, then our actions are not truly altruistic. For example, a fMRI study showed that acting kindly stimulated activity in the caudate nucleus and the anterior cingulate, which are the pleasure centers of the brain.[16] So, what should we do to act in the image of the Holy Spirit?

The first step is to recognize the person in need of help is an individual rather than part of a group. As soon as we mentally put a person into a group, the stereotypes in the heart take over and dominate our response. But science shows we can regain control with an individual focus. One fMRI study looked the amygdala, the fear center of the brain, when white participants were shown pictures of blacks. The amygdala was quiet when the participants considered them as individuals by being asked to guess what type of vegetable the person in the picture would like.[17]

We are created to compassionately connect with others and we can do this each day in many ways. The list includes a smile, respect, gratitude, touch, forgiveness, empathy, loyalty and humor.

Smile

A smile shows joy and can also show someone that you care about them. It is also good for the health of the person who smiles. Studies show that the positive attitude associated with smiling enhances our health, marriage, income, friendships and work performance.[18] For example, a study of 1952 baseball cards showed that the players who smiled on their card lived to an average age of 80 compared to the age of 73 for the others.[19] Another study found that women with a genuine smile in their college yearbook photo had better marriage stability and life satisfaction.[20]

An infant starts smiling in the womb. At eight weeks, baby girls smile much more than baby boys, a difference in average smiling frequency that continues throughout life. Smiles are universal. Unfortunately, most people smile less as they get older. This is one negative effect of aging that we can reverse. Let's smile as frequently as children.

Respect

We all need to feel that we matter, yet in today's world, importance seems to stem from what we have accomplished or who our family is. Jesus taught that each of us is important when he said "Whatever you did for one of the least of these brothers of mine, you did for me" (Matthew 25:40). Respect includes this affirmation of a person's worth, treating them politely and expressing gratitude.

Whenever we interact with someone, we should pause to recognize that they were created in the image of God and that Jesus said that He loves them. A person can sense if they are being valued, being used or being ignored, so we do not have to take specific action. A feeling of affirmation of their human dignity is so valuable, especially to someone who is troubled.

It is important to support those in a lower position than you are. Hierarchies will always exist, just as they do in the "pecking order" of the animal kingdom. Those lower in rank feel more stress, largely due to the issue of respect.[21] Unfortunately, people often put others down to build themselves up. You can do so much by exalting others. "For those who exalt themselves will be humbled, and those who humble themselves will be exalted" (Matthew 23:12).

Studies show the importance of respect in the workplace. Employees who are polite are seen as more competent and twice as likely to be viewed as leaders.[22] In another experiment, rudeness prompted a 61% decline in the ability to do word puzzles and a 58% drop in creativity. Simply witnessing the rudeness gave rise to a 22% decline in the puzzles and a 28% drop in creativity.[23]

Make an extra effort to practice respect towards Christians who do not share all of your beliefs. Despite what you see as a clear message in the Bible, other intelligent people can read the Bible and come to a different understanding. You cannot help them examine God's Word without making an effort to first understand where they are coming from.

Gratitude

Scientific studies show that offering gratitude has a strong calming effect on our bodies.[24] This includes a drop in the level of the stress hormone cortisol and increased effectiveness of our immune system. Another study found that people, who had high scores when tested for their amount of gratitude, had more energy, slept better, had higher self-efficacy (the belief in your ability to deal with a situation) and better heart health.[25]

Consider keeping a daily gratitude journal. This is an easy and effective way to significantly increase your happiness. A gratitude journal helps us appreciate some of the wonderful things God has blessed us with instead of taking them for granted.

Touch

The effectiveness of transferring our emotions through touch is much stronger than generally realized. In an interesting experiment volunteers stuck their arm out from behind a curtain so there was no visual contact with the face. Then a stranger made a light touch on their forearm for a second or two to transfer an emotion. For most emotions, the success rate was very high. However, men had a hard time recognizing anger from women and women could not recognize sympathy from men.[26] Other research shows that touch is more effective in expressing deep emotions like love than either body language or facial expressions.[27] God designed us to touch each other.

Special cells in our skin called Merkel cells are able to recognize the subtle differences in touch between emotions. Touch was designed to be an important part of how we relate to each other beyond sexual reproduction. In medieval Europe, mutual grooming such as removing head lice was the main leisure activity.[28] In our touch-deprived society, a kindergarten teacher is unable to hug a student because of potential problems with sexual abuse. Wherever touch is appropriate, get back to using it to support others.

An aversion to touch is exhibited by a Pharisee in the gospel, but Jesus rebuked him. "If this man were a prophet, he would know who is touching him and what kind of woman she is" (Luke 7:39). Jesus touched the blind and even the leper although leprosy was considered highly contagious. Jesus showed that touch was an effective way of connecting with people. We think of touching as a way of spreading germs, yet a study has found that getting more hugs decreases the number of colds we catch and the ones we catch are less severe.[29]

Infant massage provides an interesting example of the power of touch. In the United States, 14% of babies are born prematurely at an annual cost to the healthcare system of $15.5 billion. Through massage, weight gain can be improved by 47%, and mothers are just as effective in this situation as trained therapists.[30] Massage by the mothers could help the babies, help the mothers and lower costs, but many hospitals do not use this treatment. We are afraid to touch.

Forgiveness

It is a bit of a stretch to consider forgiveness as a gift since when we forgive someone we receive the greatest benefit. Forgiveness from the heart releases us from any frustration, anger, resentment, disappointment, annoyance and other negative emotions that continue to bother us after the incident. We have been designed to forgive and move on, but the process is not an easy one.

The Bible emphasizes forgiveness and Jesus forgave sins prior to healing. In the Lord's prayer, we are instructed to ask God to "Forgive us our sins as we also forgive everyone who sins against us" (Luke 11:4). The Bible even goes beyond what we think of as forgiveness. We are taught "Love your enemies and pray for those who persecute you" (Matthew 5:44). Love "keeps no record of wrongs" (1 Corinthians 13:5).

Forgiveness is about getting over the hurt of the past, but don't confuse forgiveness with reconciliation. Reconciliation may not be appropriate to the situation. For instance, a woman who is a victim of domestic assault can forgive without moving back to a situation where she risks being assaulted again.

The second issue to be clear on is fairness. Forgiveness is not about fairness and we are taught to leave the issue of fairness to God. "Do not judge, and you will not be judged. Do not condemn, and you will not be condemned. Forgive, and you will be forgiven" (Luke 6:37). We have missed the point about forgiveness if we seek to judge whether the offender's contrition is sufficient.

Accept that forgiveness is not in any way excusing, condoning or rewarding bad behavior. It is not giving the offender the power to do evil and of course, it is wrong to encourage evil. Nor is it convincing yourself that the offense did not really matter to you. Your heart will not grant you full release if you try to forgive without recognizing evil does matter and it is wrong.

Some people are more easily forgiven than others. Science shows that it is easier for us to pardon someone that we have seen as conscientious, honest, humble and/or benevolent prior to the transgression. For others, we have to work harder.

Once we are over these stumbling blocks, then we can get started. Forgiveness from the heart involves a process rather than a quick decision to forgive. Here are the four steps recommended by Robert Enright of the University of Wisconsin at Madison.

1. Self-discovery – understand your hurt and how it has affected your life.
2. Deciding to forgive – it can take time and effort to reach the stage where you decide that you would like to forgive someone.
3. Understanding – seek to understand what may have motivated the person to hurt you. Somehow their life experience led them to a bad behavior. A partial understanding of where they may be coming from is important for your heart to forgive.
4. Release – your pain from the hurt is not serving a useful purpose, so let it go. Only then will your heart be free to forgive.[31]

Whenever you have been seriously hurt, forgiveness is necessary, but difficult. It helps if you have a friend or therapist with whom you can talk things through. And do not forget to talk to God. Turning the situation over to God and trusting in Him is a powerful way to enhance forgiveness.

Whenever we have been harmed, we would like an apology. Unfortunately, apologies are usually ineffective for two reasons. For an apology to be meaningful, it needs to be unconditional and heartfelt. Most apologies are given with the implied condition that the apology somehow lessens the guilt and/or it is now time to move on. Secondly, the person committing the transgression will see it from their perspective, a perspective that is undoubtedly warped in your eyes. They will not feel the transgression is as serious as you feel it is and will have their reasons for partial justification. One scientific study showed that forgiveness is better for you without receiving an apology first[32], but more work is probably needed to confirm this finding. So do not look for or demand an apology as a condition for forgiving, but do not hesitate to apologize when you have hurt someone.

We are called to offer forgiveness for minor issues as well as when we are seriously hurt. It is often a slight from a friend or family member that is bothering us. The same rules apply to this situation. Forgiveness is a powerful gift, even after recognizing that we are giving mostly to ourselves.

Empathy

"Rejoice with those who rejoice: mourn with those who mourn" (Romans 12:15). The word empathy comes from the Greek word *empathia* which means "feeling into." It is listening to and feeling the emotion of the person speaking rather than just the words. This feeling in the heart bypasses the intellect.

Science has found that we are created with mirror neurons to allow our hearts to share feelings. For example, if we see someone eating an apple, our subconscious mind tastes the apple through these mirror neurons. If we see someone is stressed, our subconscious mind imports that stressed feeling. And if someone radiates joy, our minds share in that joy.

Empathy is at the core of how we effectively live together. "Finally, all of you, be like minded, be sympathetic, love one another, be compassionate and humble" (1 Peter 3:8). We need to feel the feelings of those around us to effectively help them.

Empathy allows us to feel what another person is feeling, while at the same time recognizing that the feelings are theirs and not ours. We also hear what the speaker is saying, but do not have to agree with it. Further, empathy does not mean that we are offering sympathy to the speaker's viewpoint or problem. Empathy means that we have heard and felt what the speaker is saying. The speaker can see that the ideas have been effectively expressed through our facial expressions and body language. Where appropriate, a gentle touch can further assist in the communication.

Science shows that we can improve our empathic abilities when we believe that we can improve and make an effort for it to be part of our personal growth.[33] When we are seeking to listen with empathy, try to listen with your whole body, pause before responding and slow down. The speaker needs to feel that you are not rushing them, you must not be anxious to chime in. In so many conversations, listeners do not hear the whole message because they are focused on how they want to reply. And try to relate at the level of the speaker. You will not connect from the heart either if you put the speaker on a pedestal or if you feel superior.

There are even special cells in our brains called mirror neurons to enhance our empathy. These were discovered by accident in Italy in 1988. Giacomo Rizzolatti was experimenting with monkeys who had thin wire electrodes inserted deep into their brains. One hot summer day, as the monkey waited in the custom-made lab chair for the research team to return from lunch, a graduate student came into the lab with an ice cream cone. When the student brought the ice cream to his mouth, the monkey's brain reacted as if the monkey itself was eating ice cream.[34]

When we receive feelings from someone else and adopt them as our own, then we have emotional contagion rather than empathy. For example, we can feel the stress from others around us, but unless we are able to recognize the stress as theirs and not ours, we will suffer the negative effects. Emotional contagion can creep into our minds without our being aware. An extreme example occurs in mob psychology where people's minds have been effectively taken over by the crowd mentality and they then act in uncharacteristic fashion.

Science shows strong health benefits from empathy, both for the speaker and the listener. When a person is in pain, deep listening has been shown to both reduce the pain and to reduce stress levels.[35] Another study recruited five multiple sclerosis patients to listen empathically to other multiple sclerosis patients. Over two years, the health of the speakers improved, but the health of the listeners improved even more.[36] And in the workplace, when managers listen with empathy, the number of sick days goes down.[37]

The power of empathy is evident in support groups that provide more than good feelings. A scientific study involving women with advanced breast cancer demonstrated this. Half of the women were randomly assigned to participate in a cancer patient support group while the other half of the patients served as the control group. Participating in a support group involved not only receiving support from other patients, but also active giving through attentive listening, empathy and compassion. Thus, the women in a support group received the health benefits that come from helping others. On average, the women in the support group lived twice as long as those who did not have the group support.[38]

There is a limit on how much empathy you should give. Aid workers are especially prone to be overwhelmed by the needs of the people that they are helping. The capacity to offer empathy differs from one person to another. Be alert regarding your limitations because when you are overwhelmed you are not helping yourself or the person in need.

A personal relationship with Jesus plays a big role in preventing burnout. Jesus was the greatest healer of all time, so consider it a privilege to serve as a healer. "I tell you, whatever you did for one of the least of these brothers and sisters of mine, you did for me" (Matthew 25:40).

If healing is your calling, recognize that you can't fix everything. Try to be empathic without letting the patient's suffering become your own. And lead a balanced life where you trust your friends and colleagues.

Loyalty

"A friend loves at all times, and a brother is born for a time of adversity" (Proverbs 17:17). When surveys look at what we desire in a potential romantic partner, loyalty often tops the list, ahead of caring, humor, honesty or intelligence. Clearly, loyalty ranks highly among the gifts we can give.

The US Marine Corps has great pride in their value-driven heritage based on loyalty. To a Marine, honor is loyalty and dedication to God, country, Corps, family and self. Their motto is Semper Fidelis, a Latin phrase that means Always Faithful.

Although corporations no longer look for employees to work in one place for life, business still understands the value of loyal employees, suppliers and customers. The companies that successfully create loyalty do so through a value-based culture.

A long-term marriage is evidence of loyalty. Science has found that those in a long-term marriage are more inclined to offer loving kindness to others.[39] This is evidence that people with loyalty share other positive traits. We all want to have people around that we know we can count on.

Humor

"Our mouths were filled with laughter and our tongues with songs of joy" (Psalm 126:2). The best humor contains an element of surprise, often an exaggeration or word play, and does not put down any person or group. It provides tremendous health benefits for both the giver and the receiver and it brings joy. When

Abraham and Sarah had a son in their old age, Sarah said, "God has brought me laughter and everyone who hears about this will laugh with me" (Genesis 21:6). They named their son Isaac, which means "laugh".

Whenever you are giving the gift of humor, be careful that it is not hurtful. Healthy laughter is infectious but jeering laughter is not. Humor requires caution. For example, an effective predictor of the strength of a marriage is if the problems are dealt with using dialogue, laughter and affection. Playful teasing between a couple is a sign of a healthy relationship, but a fine line exists between playful and hurtful.

Some benefits of laughter that science has discovered include relaxing the muscles, a decrease in the stress hormone cortisol, an increase in the immune system, the release of the pleasure molecule dopamine and improved heart health.[40] The surprise associated with humor develops the brain's creativity.[41] Thus, peek-a-boo is a great game to play with an infant.

The amount we laugh has decreased despite the health and happiness benefits that laughter brings. A German study found that in the 1940s we laughed an average of eighteen minutes a day. By the 1980s, laughter dropped to an average six minutes and today it appears to be even lower.[42] Laughter is a social response that we need. As long as you are not hurtful, humor is a gift worth giving even if people say you are not funny.

Summary

"Follow God's example, therefore, as dearly loved children and walk in the way of love" (Ephesians 5:1). The one overriding principle for giving is, just give. Science shows that the more you make heartfelt gifts, the more you will want to give. This is because God has created our minds in His image: that is, to give. Look for ways to give and recognize that giving brings you physical and emotional benefits.

A wealthy person making a major donation to a charity is not the type of gift to concentrate on. Gifts with a personal connection such as a smile, respect, gratitude, touch, forgiveness, empathy, loyalty and humor are what bring the greatest health and happiness benefits to us. Receiving these benefits requires that we give in a non-judgmental manner with a sense of caring rather than a sense of obligation.

Part 3

ALIGNING YOUR EMOTIONS TO THE IMAGE OF GOD

CHAPTER EIGHT

HOW TO BE JOYFUL ALWAYS

"Rejoice always"
(1 Thessalonians 5:16).

O ur first reaction to the Biblical teaching of "Rejoice always" is to feel that this is not possible. Of course, we will experience periods of sadness in our lives, but this does not mean the Bible is wrong. Happiness comes with strong activity in the left prefrontal cortex of our brains while sadness shows up on the right side. When our identity is living our lives in the image of God, the joyful areas in our brains remain active throughout periods of sadness.

Not only does happiness feel good, it is a requirement of the Christian life that we should work on. In this chapter, we will explore why happiness is a requirement, the types of happiness, the barriers we face in maintaining happiness and the model Jesus gave us to live by.

As we saw in the last chapter, we get personal health benefits from helping others. Science shows that people whose happiness comes largely through helping others will have better health than those who focus on personal pleasure. A study found this includes overall health, depression levels and a stronger ability of the blood to fight off infections and reduce inflammation. Inflammation is involved in many health problems such as cardiovascular disease, dementia and arthritis.[1]

Our Happiness Level is Falling

If you search Amazon.com, you will find more than 90,000 books on happiness.[2] For the most part, these books fail because they neglect to bring God into the discussion. We are living in the most prosperous economy in history, yet our happiness levels continue to drop.

A 2010 Conference Board survey in the United States showed that only 45% of workers are happy with their jobs. This number has been dropping steadily from the 61% reporting happiness with their jobs when the survey began twenty-two years earlier. In a related statistic, workers reporting that they liked their co-workers also fell from 68% to 56% during the same period.[3]

The fall in happiness has been especially prevalent with women. In the 1970s, women were happier than men. Now, men show higher happiness levels than women in the United States and in Western Europe.[4]

Being Joyful is Not an Option

When we commit to following Jesus, it means we commit to a life of lasting joy. We find a way to be joyful in whatever circumstances come our way. Through spiritual growth, our love and joy multiplies. "The Lord is my strength and my shield; my heart trusts in Him, and He helps me. My heart leaps for joy" (Psalm 28:7).

Somehow the idea that our spiritual life should focus on our personal joy does not feel right. Jesus sacrificed Himself on the cross for us, so our sense of fairness cries out for us to sacrifice. The focus on joy seems selfish and wrong, at least that is what Satan says through the reward illusion.

Nothing we can do will compensate for many blessings God has granted us. So leave the issues of fairness to God and look at the five reasons to focus on joy.

- Scripture tells us to be joyful. "Joy" is mentioned over two hundred times in the Bible and "rejoice" over two hundred times. A disciple of Jesus follows His teachings.

- We must embrace the Holy Spirit. In Biblical times, the concept of first fruits was important. The first fruits of the harvest were considered special and offered to the temple. The firstfruits of the Holy Spirit are love and joy. "The fruit of the Spirit is love, joy, peace, forbearance, kindness, goodness, faithfulness, gentleness and self-control" (Galatians 5:22). Unless we embrace love and joy, we are not embracing the Holy Spirit.

- Joy is a force that changes our hearts. When we feel joy associated with Christian values, it solidifies those values. Without joy, all the intellectual effort we put forward towards altering our minds will not be effective.

- Joy inspires. Our joy supports other Christians and helps to bring people to Jesus. Good news brings joy so we should share it to others. Jesus said "I must proclaim the good news of the kingdom of God" (Luke 4:43).

- Our willpower is simply too weak to maintain active growth towards enhancing ourselves in the image of God unless there is joy in this path.

"Ask and it will be given to you; seek and you will find" (Luke 11:9). Joy is one of the goals we should seek in a proactive fashion rather than simply waiting for the occasional burst of joy to come upon us. The joy we seek goes beyond an effervescent mood. Jesus said "Ask and you will receive, and your joy will be complete" (John 16:24). So let us explore what it means for our joy to be complete.

The Types of Happiness

For many years, scientific research on the human mind focused almost exclusively on understanding problems such as diseases and negative emotions. In recent years, however, the research community has taken a serious look at positive emotions. Science wants to understand what makes us happy as evidenced by the International Positive Psychology Association that attracts more than two thousand researchers to its annual conference.

Science has identified three main types of happiness: hedonic which is the happiness that we feel from pleasure, flow which is the happiness we feel when our mind is actively engaged and eudaimonic which is the happiness from doing something meaningful.[5] The three types of happiness fit the three natural priorities of the mind–meeting our basic needs gives us pleasure, thinking clearly engages our mind and helping others brings meaning.

We also find joy in remembering positive experiences from our past. This can be the taste of a special meal, the steps we took to achieve something or the joy someone received from your loving help. Sometimes, anticipation also brings these positive feelings.

Through perverse logic, sinful pleasures are often seen as bringing joy and God is seen as standing in the way of us enjoying ourselves. This elevates sin to a status that it does not deserve. And using our willpower to resist the sin makes the sin even more appealing. Once we realize that God offers us far greater joy in this life, the power of sin wilts away. "The prospect of the righteous is joy, but the hopes of the wicked come to nothing" (Proverbs 10:28).

Pleasure – The Happiness from Meeting our Basic Needs

"Whoever loves pleasure will become poor; whoever loves wine and oil will never be rich" (Proverbs 21:17). Our bodies are designed to feel pleasure when we meet a basic need such as enjoying a drink of cool water when we are thirsty or cozying up to a fireplace when we are cold. But we frequently fall victim to the illusion that even more of what we require will give us more happiness.

Drug addiction is a good example of how the mind is easily trained for pleasure. The first exposure to the drug provides a rush or the addict would not continue. However, the highs that the drug brings are offset by the lows when the addict craves another hit. There is no net pleasure gained from the drug, while the life of the addict can be devastating.

Science shows that the amount of pleasure that we receive over our lifetime has a fixed upper limit. It varies from person to person because of genetics, but you cannot increase it.[6] Like the drug addict, a life spent seeking hedonistic pleasure does not bring a net increase in pleasure.

Our inability to get more pleasure from financial wealth is another finding about human nature that is difficult to believe. Lottery winners revert back to their previous happiness level after a couple of months.[7] This research certainly upsets the gambling industry. Unfortunately, we falsely assume that even if that may be the case for other people, if we won the lottery we would be an exception. Ways to increase your happiness exist, but seeking it through a pleasurable lifestyle does not work.

It is easy to be confused about how to find true happiness. The Bible is telling us to be joyful and then science teaches us that it is not possible to get past our genetically-induced pleasure level. The answer is to reduce the barriers to our happiness and also to seek the other two forms of happiness. "Those that live according to the flesh have their minds set on what the flesh desires; but those who live in accordance with the Spirit have their minds set on what the Spirit desires" (Romans 8:5).

Engagement – The Happiness from Thinking Clearly

Engagement is the type of happiness we feel when our mind is fully occupied in an activity to the point where our mind does not wander. Engagement fits with the second priority of the subconscious mind of thinking clearly. It can be achieved through an active event like rock climbing or a passive event like getting lost in a movie. Training can improve the level of happiness we experience through engagement. The state of flow, as discussed in Chapter 6, is the strongest form of engagement and thus brings the greatest amount of this type of happiness.

Our minds are usually wandering too much to feel the joy of being fully engaged in an activity. A study looked at 250,000 responses from 2,200 volunteers using an iPhone app to show how deeply they were engaged in an activity. It showed that 47% of the time their minds were wandering to something other than what they were doing. The study found that the most focused activity was sexual intercourse where a 90% engagement occurred.[8]

We also have a type of engagement when our identity is living in the image of God. Then, we have a joyful feeling of serenity. This serenity is a powerful inner peace that comes from the Holy Spirit. After love and joy, the third fruit of the Holy Spirit is peace (Galatians 5:22). We seek His help through prayers such as the serenity prayer developed by Reinhold Niebuhr (and subsequently modified and used by Alcoholics Anonymous): "God grant me the serenity to accept the things I cannot change. Courage to change the things I can change. And wisdom to know the difference."

Meaning – The Happiness from Helping Others

Research has shown that the most effective way to increase your happiness is through a meaningful life. It is simply the right thing to do. The Holy Spirit is available and ready to help you in this.

We often mistakenly think the meaningful life is measured in grand accomplishments, like Billy Graham preaching the gospel to millions and leading countless people to Jesus. Of course, this type of success for God is important. We can learn from the lives of these people, but for most of us, that is not what God is calling us to do.

We are created in the image of our loving God. We are called to let that image shine. It is the simple things that we can offer to everyone we connect with that make the most difference. A smile, an affirmation or an unexpected kindness will bring happiness to both you and to the fortunate recipient.

Barriers to Joy

Many barriers stand in the way of us living the life of joy, but if they are recognized and worked on, then we can minimize their effect.

Low Self-Esteem

You can't have lasting joy if you do not feel good about yourself. Recognize that you are created in the image of God. With the grace of the Holy Spirit, you are on the path to renewing the glory of your human nature. You are important to God.

Other People

Our minds have been created in the image of our loving God to love other people. "Love your neighbor as yourself" (Mark 12:31). Since our minds desire engaging with others, it follows that we will be disappointed if they react badly to us. But if we follow the teachings of Jesus, we will not let the reactions of other people rob us of our joy.

We recognize that people will criticize us from time to time, but we simply accept that as part of life. We listen to what they say because there may be a growth opportunity for us in their words. However, we will not let them deflect us from doing God's will.

If we base the joy of our spirit on the reactions of other people, then they can take it from us. If our joy is based on the wonderful opportunity Jesus has given us to follow Him, then our joy is secure. Love and joy are the firstfruits of the Holy Spirit. We do not need to allow bad behavior from others to steal our joy.

Difficulties in Marriage

If you are seeking to improve your marriage, let God do it. When a couple puts God first, happiness soars and the interest in divorce disappears. That is the finding of the 2011 University of Virginia survey report for the National Marriage Project.

Marital satisfaction was measured in over 1,000 couples aged 18-46 with children and then the standard statistical adjustments were made for age, education, income and ethnicity. They found that when both spouses made God the center of their marriage, the percentage reporting that the marriage was very happy jumped from 50% to 77% for women and from 50% to 76% for men.[9]

The Illusions of Money, Fame and Power

The selfish illusion says that more money, fame or power will not make us happier, but because this is a powerful illusion, we do not believe that this would be the case for us. When we compare a primitive society to billionaires, we see that money does not matter. The Maasai live in small, remote villages in East Africa. Their homes are built of mud, dung and sticks. Their culture does not include amenities that we take for granted like running water and electricity. Yet when their happiness is tested, they are on par with American billionaires.[10]

Although we feel that more money will make us happier, it is simply not true. On average, the people in Costa Rica are happier than those in the United States or Western Europe even though their per capita GDP is a tenth of the more developed counties.[11] Another study of 6,200 lawyers found that junior partners in prestigious law firms were just as happy as their high-income senior partners. And public service lawyers are happier even though they make much less money.[12] Science has consistently found that wealth levels make no difference to happiness, except for the destitute. Happiness does go down if you do not have enough food to eat or a roof over your head.

We often dream of an opulent lifestyle and have been conditioned to believe that this will make us happier. If we live our lives based on lifestyle, our joy is lost in every setback. And if we do reach our goal, we can find it is empty. So then we typically decide that the bar was not set high enough and that the solution is to achieve even greater wealth. Do not let this illusion rob you of the joy of your daily life.

"I know what it is to have plenty. I have learned the secret of being content in any and every situation, whether well fed or hungry, whether living in plenty or in want" (Philippians 4:12). Of course, the "secret" is following the teaching of Jesus.

Time

It is easy to get too busy. So many things that we feel that we need to get done or would like to accomplish do not really matter. Would they be a concern to the Maasai? Would they be a concern to the people of Costa Rica?

When you analyze it, many "to do" items concern your identity and it is not an identity in the image of God. It is an identity concerned with what other people think about you. Whenever time is a big concern, ask God for serenity. Try making a to do list that eliminates tasks that are not really necessary. Then you will have time to do God's will and experience the joy that He offers us.

Worry

Scientists use the term "affective forecasting" when they explore how accurately we can predict our emotional response to a future event. Their research shows that our minds are very poor at it. The actual emotional response to a future event tends to be much lower than what we anticipate.[13]

Part of the reason we over-estimate the future emotional response is that our minds focus on the event and ignore the various other things that will be going on at the same time. These other factors tend to reduce the negative emotion of the event itself. Another reason is that our heart has what scientists have called a "psychological immune system" that lets us cope with events by blunting their effects.

Worrying about something that may or may not happen in the future does not solve anything and adds stress to your life. It robs you of the joy of the moment. "I tell you, do not to worry about your life" (Matthew 6:25).

Health

It is difficult to be joyful when you are in pain or have received a negative health diagnosis. Whatever your medical condition is, positive emotions will help the healing process, while stress and negative emotions make healing more difficult. So when you have a health problem, find something that makes you laugh. Science shows that laughter is beneficial therapy.[14] And it makes those around you feel better as well. Of course, laughter will not heal every health problem, but the reduction of the stress level through laughter will help your body heal itself. "A cheerful heart is good medicine, but a crushed spirit dries up the bones" (Proverbs 17:22).

Several studies have shown that a positive attitude will enhance your life expectancy, including a striking analysis of a group of nuns. In 1930, the Mother Superior of the Sisters of Notre Dame requested that each sister write a short autobiographical sketch of her life when she took her vows. Here are a couple of examples written in 1932:

"God started my life off well by bestowing upon me grace of inestimable value... The past year which I spent as a candidate studying at Notre Dame has been a very happy one. Now I look forward with eager joy to receiving the Holy Habit of Our Lady and to a life of union with Love divine." Cecilia O'Payne

"I was born on September 26, 1909, the eldest of seven children, five girls and two boys...My candidate year was spent in the mother-house, teaching chemistry and second year Latin at Notre Dame Institute. With God's grace, I intend to do my best for our Order, for the spread of religion and for my personal sanctification" Marguerite Donnely

Researchers divided the 180 nuns who had written a sketch into four groups based on how much joy was expressed in their writing. This was an excellent sample for statistical analysis because they were all female, all had the same diet, all were single, none of them smoked or drank heavily, all had the same medical care and they all lived within the same social support network. The researchers compared lifespan with the joy expressed in the sketch.

By the age of 85, 90% of the most cheerful group was still alive but only 34% of the least cheerful group made it. At age 94, the results were even more striking...54% compared with 11%. Sister Cecelia, who wrote "very happy" and "eager joy," lived to age 98 while Sister Marguerite, who expressed no joy in her life sketch, died at 59.[15]

Another nun, Sister Candida Bellotti, spoke to journalists after meeting with Pope Francis on her 107th birthday. She said "Only those who feel the happiness of drawing near to the Lord can understand how abundant His love for us is, and how much serenity He leaves in our hearts."

Emotional Contagion

As discussed in Chapter Six, we have mirror neurons that allow us to feel the emotions of other people. As long as we are able to recognize that these emotions we pick up belong to someone else and are not our own, the empathy we offer through sharing them is very valuable. The danger comes when the other person's negative emotions dominate our mind. If we are mindful of the danger and tell ourselves that we are not going to take ownership of the negative emotion, then we come a long way towards keeping our joyful attitude.

Emotional contagion works both ways. Our joy is picked up by others and soothes their negative feelings. When we radiate joy and identify ourselves as Christians, we encourage others to follow Jesus.

Unfairness

We have been created with a strong instinct for fairness as explored with the reward illusion in Chapter 1. To determine fairness, we have to judge a situation. "Do not judge, or you too will be judged" (Matthew 7:1). We simply do not know God's plan for another person. When we invoke the idea of fairness, we are sometimes making a judgement based on incomplete information.

Leave the judgement to God. We are taught to love our neighbor (Mark 12:31). Jesus died on the cross for us, which is the most unfair situation of all. So put your trust in God and let Him handle any question of fairness. "I have fought the good fight, I have finished the race, I have kept the faith. Now there is in store for me the crown of righteousness, which the Lord, the righteous judge, will award to me on that day—and not only to me, but also to all who have longed for His appearing" (2 Timothy 4:7-8).

Nick Vujicic is an Australian who was born without any arms or legs. Instead of letting his disability limit his life, Nick travels the world as an inspirational Christian speaker. He wrote a book titled Life Without Limits, Inspiration for a Ridiculously Good Life and challenges us to: "take a moment to think about any limitations you've placed on your life or that you've allowed others to place

101

on it. Now think about what it would be like to be free of those limitations. What would your life be if anything were possible?"[16]

Grief

When loved ones lose their lives, we mourn their lost opportunities. Sometimes we feel an element of unfairness exists. We are sad because they are no longer available to us. And it just does not feel right to be joyful at these times.

Of course, it would be heartless not to feel a loss. Leave the issues of fairness to God and focus on all the joy that the loved one brought into the world. Thank God for allowing them to be part of your life. Death lets us appreciate how wonderful life really is. So maintain that quiet joy.

Guilt

If guilt is holding you back from your Christian joy, then put the issue behind you and recognize that guilt leading to repentance makes you a better person. Science shows that guilt can be more effective than the fear of negative consequences in guiding our moral behavior.[17] If possible, apologize to a person you have wronged. Ask God for forgiveness since God is merciful and forgives our sins.

The fact that your conscience makes you feel guilty means that you care about others. So label yourself as a good person that is created in the image of God and growing in the Holy Spirit, rather than as a failure. Your conscience can aid your growth mindset as you seek to improve. Whenever you feel guilt, it is an excellent time to repent and open your heart to the Holy Spirit for Him to bring His firstfruits of love and joy.

Sometimes a distinction is made between the meanings of guilt and shame as it relates to our identity. A person with a righteous identity feels guilt when making a mistake, but retains the identity of a righteous person. However, a person feeling shame loses the righteous feeling. As we saw in Chapter 2, it is vital for a Christian to accept the teaching in the Bible and retain the righteous identity despite making mistakes.

Regret

We can always look back and see our failures. It is never too late to dedicate your life to Jesus and receive the love and joy that He has waiting for us. So reflect on the works of Paul, "I do not consider myself yet to have taken hold of it. But one thing I do: Forgetting what is behind and straining towards what is ahead" (Philippians 3:13). Paul was a Pharisee who persecuted Christians. Surely, his cause for regret would have been greater than yours.

It is the sincerity of repentance before God that makes the difference, rather than the severity of guilt. When Paul wrote "forgetting what is behind", he did not mean to imply forgetting the debt of love that he owed. He is teaching us to go forward with confidence because we have a new beginning with the grace of God.

Self-Inflicted Suffering

Historically, many Christians have inflicted suffering on themselves seeking to get closer to Jesus. For example, Martin Luther tried to get closer to God through sacrifice during his early days as a hermit monk. He said, "I lost touch with Christ the Savior and Comforter, and made of Him the jailor and hangman of my poor soul." It is perverse logic to feel that these self-inflicted sacrifices make us more worthy, but again the reward illusion plays havoc with our priorities.

If we wish to follow Jesus, we must follow the path He has set out which involves joy. Otherwise, we are not following Him. God wants us to radiate his love and joy so that others will be attracted to the Christian faith. "When you fast, put oil on your head and wash your face, so that it will not be obvious to others that you are fasting" (Matthew 6:17-18).

There are reasons why we undergo discomfort such as actively training our body for an upcoming competition. And, there are significant health benefits from intermittent fasting. Just don't assume that God delights in our suffering.

Follow the Example of Jesus

The Bible shows us that Jesus lived a life of joy. He says that He was described as "The Son of Man came eating and drinking, and they say, 'Here is a glutton and a drunkard, a friend of tax collectors and sinners'" (Matthew 11:19). His first public miracle was to turn water into high quality wine at a wedding feast. Jesus was fully human and engaged in human pleasures.

Jesus liked to use humor. A light hidden under a bowl (Matthew 5:15), a house built on sand (Matthew 7:26-27) or throwing pearls to pigs (Matthew 7:6) were humorous examples that He used to illustrate important points. When Jesus taught, He made the people listening feel good and that added to the effectiveness of His communication.

Jesus also brought joy through meaningful actions. His miracles involved helping people such as feeding a large crowd or healing the sick. He showed courage and compassion when He stood up to the Pharisees and saved a woman from being stoned, which brought joy to the woman he saved (John 8:1-11).

Summary

Our personal happiness is something we should actively be working on. That statement sounds like license to engage in hedonistic delights, but science shows hedonism does not make us happier. Our minds have a fixed amount of pleasure they will register. Getting that pleasure from one source decreases the amount available through other sources.

Instead, increased happiness comes from a meaningful life where we help others. This is also the type of happiness that improves our health. So, we should work on those factors that may be holding us back from achieving the happiness that God's plan for us entails.

In the final analysis, the love we find through helping others is what leads to the complete joy that Jesus teaches. As we grow in our ability to love, we also grow our ability to feel Christian joy. "If you keep my commands, you will remain in my love, just as I have kept my Father's commands and remain in His love. I have told you this so that my joy may be in you and that your joy may be complete. My command is this: Love each other as I have loved you" (John 15:10-12).

CHAPTER NINE

MOTIVATION IN THE IMAGE OF GOD

"For the Spirit God gave us
does not make us timid, but gives us power,
love and self-discipline"

(2 Timothy 1:7).

W e all have goals, even if these goals are not clearly identified, and we all struggle from time to time with our motivation. The goals can be either extrinsic or intrinsic. Extrinsic goals are things like wealth, fame, power, appearance or pleasure. Intrinsic goals come from the heart and are related to the way we are created in the image of God.

A scientific study showed that meeting an intrinsic goal improves our psychological health while attaining extrinsic goals relate to negative consequences. The study measured satisfaction, self-esteem, positive emotions and physical symptoms such as headache and anxiety.[1]

As we have previously seen with the control illusion, our intellect is not in control the way we think it is. Since is far more activity is taking place in the heart than in the conscious mind, the heart can dominate our motivation. "I do not understand what I do. For what I want to do, I do not do, but what I hate I do" (Romans 7: 15).

Money Is an Overrated Motivator

The selfish illusion, where we seek things like material goods, recognition or hedonistic pleasure beyond our basic needs is an illusion of the intellect. Most people believe that external rewards such as wealth accumulation are the dominant motivators. Thus, the science shows us something about human nature that is somewhat counter-intuitive. Before we look at what motivates us, we will discuss research that shows money is not a primary driver of our actions.

"Keep your lives free from the love of money and be content with what you have" (Hebrews 13:5). The world believes that the way to enhance productivity is to increase financial incentives. Despite more and more studies showing that this is not a good way to motivate people, the world continues to ignore the scientific findings. It is easier to ignore evidence than to embrace an idea that seems illogical.

The Federal Reserve Bank commissioned a study to test this radical theory. Four leading economists were commissioned to conduct various tests in the United States and rural India. India was selected because among poorer people the financial rewards would be extremely significant to the participants.

The testing used a variety of tasks that included creativity, motor skills and concentration. The participants were divided into three groups according to the incentive they would receive (low pay, medium pay and high pay). Results showed that high money reward brought a lower performance in both the United States and India.[2]

The discovery that rewards could hurt performance was first made back in 1949 when it was observed that monkeys would solve puzzles faster if they were not given a food reward for their success.[3] People also solve puzzles faster if they are not rewarded.[4] Many studies now confirm this radical idea including the finding that paying for blood donations caused a reduction in the blood supply[5] and that fines for late pick-up at daycare caused more late pick-ups.[6] Sam Bowles of the Santa Fe Institute analyzed fifty-one corporate studies and found overwhelming evidence that financial incentives reduced performance.[7]

There are two important cautions before we suggest that financial remuneration is an ineffective motivator. First, remuneration must be sufficient for the employee to meet their basic needs. Meeting your basic needs is the first priority of the mind and employees will be troubled if they are unable to pay for food and rent.

The second caution is that remuneration must be seen as fair. As we saw in Chapter 4, our minds have a strong inclination towards fairness. For example, scientists see the reaction to unfairness even in sixteen-month infants.[8] So whatever the level of compensation, it will be a problem if employees feel unfairness either relative to industry norms or relative to other employees.

Intrinsic Motivation

Science has found that intrinsic motivation is more powerful than external motivation. The leading scientific explanation about how we are motivated is called Self-determination Theory. This theory is well-established among professors around the world and conferences on this topic attract over 500 researchers.

The Self-determination Theory states that our intrinsic motivation is based on autonomy, competence and relatedness. As we can see below, this is essentially the same thing as the three natural priorities of the mind—to meet our basic needs, to think clearly and to help others. So the scientific understanding of intrinsic motivation relates directly to how we are created in the image of God.

Bestselling authors have modified the three factors and in doing so have diverged from what is taught in academic circles. Daniel Pink wrote we are driven by autonomy, mastery and purpose[9] while Tom Rath uses the terms energy, interaction and meaning.[10] The academic understanding matches best with how we are created in the image of God.

Autonomy

"Do you not know that your bodies are temples of the Holy Spirit, who is in you, whom you have received from God? You are not your own; you were bought at a price. Therefore, honor God with your body" (1 Corinthians 6:19-20). Autonomy stems from our basic desire to take care of ourselves. When we are born, we are totally dependent on caregivers to meet our basic needs. As we grow, we want to learn to do things ourselves. Obviously, life would not work out if everyone tried to rely on their parents for all their needs after reaching adulthood.

The instinct to care for ourselves spills over into our preference to have some control over the things that we do. For example, in the business world employees are more productive when given more autonomy unless the job is so basic that no creative thinking is required.

Competence

"I can do all this through Him who gives me strength" (Philippians 4:13). Our minds like to engage in activities where we are competent. Competency allows us to get into the flow of an activity without the second-guessing and confusion we find when we are just learning or not proficient. Thus, competence allows us to think clearly, which is also the second natural priority of the mind.

As we are developing skills or understanding, we get confused from time to time. This is a normal part of growth. Recognize that new skills come with a learning curve and that our minds will have better flow as our competence improves. If you are feeling down because of a failure, consider what the following people went through:

- Dismissed from drama school with a note that said she was too shy to put her best foot forward – Lucille Ball
- Turned down by the Deca music company with the comment that "we don't like your sound and guitar music is on the way out" – The Beatles
- Cut from the high school basketball team, he went home to his room and cried – Michael Jordan
- Told by a teacher that he was too stupid to learn anything and that he should go into a field where he could succeed by virtue of the pleasant personality – Thomas Edison
- Fired from a newspaper because he lacked imagination and had no original ideas – Walt Disney
- Defeated in eight elections and had a nervous breakdown – Abraham Lincoln

Relatedness

"Let us consider how we may spur one another on toward love and good deeds, not giving up meeting together, as some are in the habit of doing, but let us encouraging one another" (Hebrews 10:24-25). We are motivated to do things where we can engage with other people. The third natural priority of the mind is to help others. The desire to help is essentially the same thing as the desire to engage with others. When we are in a group, we do not want to be seen as a just a taker, but want to contribute.

Our motivation is stronger when we are working as part of a team than when we are trying to achieve something by ourselves. As a team member, we put in that extra effort so as not to let down the team or to achieve something with them.

When you make a plan, it is more effective when you share the details of your plan. The act of telling someone and letting them monitor your progress involves them in your objective and thus puts them on your team. You are then more committed to successfully complete your plan. Scripture tells us to "encourage one another daily" (Hebrews 3:13).

Billy Graham compared his team at the Billy Graham Evangelical Association to a professional baseball team. He then went on to praise his team members. He says that his team competed against Satan.[11]

Motivation is difficult when we consider ourselves to be the central issue. It is much easier when we realize that we are part of a much bigger plan. That is what Jesus meant when He taught that we must lose our lives for Him.

Shape the task for intrinsic motivation

Sometimes we can shape a task to enhance intrinsic motivation. For example, working hard for a vacation with a loving spouse is more motivating than working hard for money. Another example is to make it a team effort so that you are helping each other. Unless the task involves some level of intrinsic motivation, ask yourself why you are doing it.

Summary

Extrinsic motivation uses willpower and frequently fails to properly motivate us. The selfish illusion leads us to think we are motivated by money, recognition or hedonistic pleasures, but we are easily distracted from such an objective. There is a better way since willpower is weak.

Intrinsic motivation, which comes from the way we are created in the image of God, is driven by the natural priorities of the heart.

These are to meet our basic needs, to think clearly and to help others. So if you are hungry, anxious or part of a team, it is easier to find motivation to meet a basic need than a task that relies on willpower. Motivation is more effective whenever a task can be framed so that the motivation comes from the heart.

FIND GOD THROUGH YOUR TROUBLES

"You of little faith? So do not worry"
(Matthew 6:30-31).

We see so much evil, pain and unfairness in the world and wonder why God allows it. The answers to these problems are complex, but we know God is there to help us. And He can help us grow through our ordeals.

Medical science has identified three symptom clusters associated with severe stress. Each symptom cluster shows what happens when we are estranged from one of the three ways we are created in the image of God. This chapter will explore the twelve ways to effectively cope with stress. It will also discuss growth coming from our troubles and how that relates to the image of God.

The Biology of Stress

Any negative thought causes stress, which in turn kills brain cells. The thoughts may also be held in our memories, which can come back and cause further problems. Fortunately, God has given us many ways to cope with our problems. The Christian mindset of love, joy and growth allows our minds to grow and flourish rather than losing their capacity through stress.

Misconceptions about the Brain

Until about the year 2000, science believed that we went through our lives with a fixed number of neurons in our brain. When these cells died, science taught that we had to carry on with fewer brain cells. Along with that, a popular myth tells us that we only use a small portion of our brain. Both ideas have proven to be myths.

We now know that our brain cells can increase or die off like other cells in our body. In many ways, brain cells behave like muscle cells. Areas of the brain can enlarge and areas can wither. Science came up with a big word for this newly recognized ability of the brain to grow new cells–neuroplasticity.

Injury to part of the brain can be compared to an injury to an arm muscle. Unless the injury is very severe, the arm can still be moved. Recovery takes time and the proper support. Each part of the brain has a specific function. When a part is injured, its function will be compromised.

The Stress Response

Stress is our body's call to action. The heart pumps more blood and our blood flow can go from one gallon per minute to five gallons per minute. Energy from carbohydrates and fats is metabolized. At the same time, energy is diverted away from our immune system so we are more susceptible to infections. Blood is diverted away from the digestive system so that digestion is put on hold while we attend to whatever is bothering us. In the short term, we make adjustments to deal with the stressful situation either by fighting or running away.[1]

The stress response is intended to be a healthy, short-term reaction to a situation. However, if the stress goes on for too long or if the stress is so strong that it overwhelms the body, then we experience a brain injury that is called trauma. Stress affects our memory, our mood and other mental functions. Neurons die while the production of new ones is significantly reduced. The most dramatic effect is seen in the hippocampus, the part of the brain responsible for short-term memory. Stress causes the hippocampus to shrink. (Failing short term memory from a reduction in the size of the hippocampus is also associated with dementia.[2]) We need to get our negative emotions, our stress and our trauma under control as soon as possible to give our minds the best chance to heal.

Categories of Stress Symptoms

According to the fourth edition of the American Psychiatric Association's Diagnostic and Statistical Manual (DSM), three symptom clusters are associated with Post-Traumatic Stress Disorder (PTSD). These three categories are also useful to understand stress when it has not reached the level of PTSD since the stress is still harmful. The three categories are reflective of an upset in one of the three natural priorities of the mind.

The first category is called re-experiencing. God created us in His image for everlasting life with Him. The first natural priority of the mind is to protect this gift of life. Whenever our life or the basic needs of life are threatened, fear takes an emotional toll on our mind. The re-experiencing cluster can involve recurrent and intrusive thoughts about the event, emotional feelings as if the event is recurring and nightmares about the event. Cues associated with the event can cause intense distress. In extreme cases, the stress can lead to hallucinations.

The second category is called hyperarousal. Because we are created in God's image with the gift of wisdom, the second natural priority of the mind is to think clearly. Stress can disrupt the way we view our life and thereby confuse the thought process. This produces symptoms such as difficulties falling and staying asleep, problems concentrating, an exaggerated response when you are startled, irritability, anger, hypervigilance, self-destructive behavior such as excess drinking and overblown feelings of guilt or shame. The mind is on edge because it is confused.

The final category is called avoidance. In His image, God gave us a loving nature. Stress can cause a feeling of detachment and even estrangement from others as we lose interest in activities. We want to avoid anything that may be associated with the stress. We lose our hope for the future. Feelings such as love and joy are simply not there. In short, we have emotionally shut down. Note that in 2013, the fifth edition of DSM expanded the symptom clusters by essentially making avoidance of anything related to the event and avoidance of unrelated activities into separate symptom clusters.

Sometimes, we do not realize how much stress has affected us. A study was done on people within 1.5 miles of the World Trade Center when the planes crashed on September 11. None had been diagnosed with PTSD, nor did they show any clinical signs of depression or anxiety. Yet four years after the crash, their brains were different from brains of the control participants. When viewing faces that showed fear, their amygdala (the brain center for negative emotions) had significantly more activity than with control participants. Further, interviews showed more psychological difficulties than the control participants. Problems included difficulty sleeping, hypervigilance, avoidance, recurrent distressing memories and bad dreams. This stress occurred simply because these people were in New York City on September 11, 2001.[3]

God's Answer to Stress

God has given us many tools to cope with stressful events that can help lead to growth when we overcome the difficulties. The three strongest ways of getting closer to God are through prayer, enhancing our wisdom through Scripture and sharing the love of the Holy Spirit. We should actively use all of them. Place a special focus on prayer if you have symptoms in the re-experiencing category, Scripture to deal with hyperarousal with its associated confusion and sharing love to deal with avoidance.

Prayer

Studies show that quiet prayer is very effective in reducing our stress levels. Even when you are very busy, pause for a moment of prayer. Jesus found time for prayer.

The ability to be still is an important trait that we struggle with. Cultivate the skill. I have found that simply taking one minute to meditate does wonders to relieve short-term stress. Longer meditative prayer sessions bring a greater sense of peace and joy. "Be still, and know that I am God" (Psalm 46:10).

God provides grace to help us get through our difficulties. Today's grace is available today and tomorrow, He will send tomorrow's grace. Ask for His grace each day.

Give Your Stress to Jesus

A prayer that will help relieve your stress is to trust in God and give your troubles to Jesus as he instructed. "Come to me all of you who are weary and burdened, and I will give you rest. Take my yoke upon you and learn from me, for I am gentle and humble in heart, and you will find rest for your souls. For my yoke is easy and my burden is light" (Matthew 11:28-30).

The primary message of the Bible is the good news of love and joy. We are created in the image of God, He wants to help with our stress, so give it to Him.

"And why do you worry about clothes. See how the lilies of the field grow. They do not labor or spin. Yet I tell you that not even Solomon in all his splendor was dressed like one of these. If that is how God clothes the grass of the field, which is here today and tomorrow is thrown into the fire, will he not much more clothe you — you of little faith? So do not worry saying 'What shall we eat?' or 'What shall we drink' or 'What shall we wear?' For the pagans run after all these things, and your heavenly Father knows that you need them. But seek first His kingdom and His righteousness, and all these things will be given to you as well. Therefore, do not worry about tomorrow, for tomorrow will worry about itself. Each day has enough trouble of its own" (Matthew 6:28-34).

Louis Zamperini was an American track star who competed at the 1936 Olympic Games and held the American Collegiate record for the mile run over a 15-year period. During WWII, his plane crashed in the Pacific Ocean and he spent 47 days adrift at sea. When his raft came ashore, he was captured by the Japanese and subjected to sadistic torture. By the time Louis returned from the war, he had severe PTSD including re-experiencing his trauma in recurring nightmares. He used alcohol to escape the torment. His wife got him to go to a Billy Graham Crusade and there he committed his life to Jesus. When Louis put his trust in Jesus, both his drinking and his nightmares stopped instantly. Louis went on to become an inspirational Christian speaker and to run a Christian camp.[4]

Seek Wisdom

The confusion caused by stress leads to more stress, so the solution needs to include getting your mind to think clearly. Jesus taught us how to think, so use His wisdom. Look at what Jesus said: "Peace I leave with you; my peace I give you. I do not give to you as the world gives. Do not let your hearts be troubled and do not be afraid" (John 14:27).

Share the Love of the Holy Spirit

An effective way to relieve stress is to do good. So with the help of the Holy Spirit, do something nice for someone. Remember that the firstfruits of the Holy Spirit are love and joy. If you approach others in the spirit of love and joy, your personal stress tends to melt away. We are created for relationships.

Accept your Role on God's Team

God created you in His image and has a plan for you. That makes you important. Unless you have clear bearings on your role and purpose, your life will be plagued with insecurity and you will question your place in the world.

God is the captain of the team. Sometimes we wait patiently for his call as if we are sitting on the bench and other times we are actively in the field of play. We conduct our lives according to His command. "Love the Lord your God with all your heart and with all your soul and with all your mind. This is the first and greatest commandment. And the second is like it: "Love your neighbor as yourself" (Matthew 22:37-39).

Unless we have a clear sense of who we are, then we will be anxiously trying to conform to what others expect us to be. Insecurity results since we feel coerced to deal with others' expectations.

This comes back to your self-image. If you believe that your basic nature is sinful because you are simply a selfish creature, you can expect a life of excess stress as you pursue your selfish goals. Unfortunately, much of the secular world believes this. Alternately, if you believe that you are created in the image of God along with the goodness that entails, you look forward to God implementing His plan through you. You approach whatever comes your way with a mindset of love, joy and growth and the stress to prove yourself just melts away.

Decide Who You Are Trying to Please

"I seek not to please myself, but Him who sent me" (John 5:30). We have been conditioned to base our actions on how other people react to us. The only one who really matters is God. When we allow ourselves to be pressured by whatever others want, we lose our sense of purpose–that is, the purpose to do God's will.

The command Jesus gave us is to give unconditional love. Unconditional love does not concern itself with pleasing the recipient to receive favor in return. Often unconditional love is reciprocated, but when we base our actions on whether or not it will be returned, then the love is no longer unconditional.

Talk to Someone You Trust

Seth Pollack of the University of Wisconsin-Madison did a stress study with a group of seven to twelve-year-old girls. The stress level was raised by having the girls give an impromptu speech and then do math problems in front of a group of strangers. After the test, one-third of the girls met their mothers, one-third spoke by phone to their mothers and one-third served as a control group by watching a non-emotional video.

The study found that contact with the mother significantly reduced the level of the stress hormone cortisol and significantly raised the level of oxytocin. Oxytocin is a hormone related to emotional bonding and trust. It made little difference if the contact was by phone or in person. This study points out the value of speaking to someone you trust after a stressful experience.[5]

Plan

While we must remain open for changes in direction, a clear plan substantially reduces stress in our lives. It is very easy to fill our lives with "busy work" and then stress about how much more is left to do.

A plan allows you forget about activities until they appear in the plan, so you do not worry about them. It is a good idea to start each day with a clear understanding of both the priorities for the day and an idea of when in the day you will attend to them. An ideal plan includes time for some fun.

Focus

Throughout the day, distractions will come your way as you seek to implement your plan. While some must be attended to and may require a change of plan, most can be ignored or quickly dealt with.

People tried to distract Jesus from spreading His message, but he refused to be deterred. In the same way, do not lose focus on your priorities. "The people were looking for Him and when they came to where He was, they tried to keep Him from leaving them. But He said, 'I must proclaim the good news of the kingdom of God to the other towns also, because that is why I was sent'" (Luke 4:42-43).

Another advantage of focus is that trying to do several things at once causes stress. And focus may save you the stress of dealing with bad decisions made from doing multiple tasks at once. A study found that when a person multitasks with two activities that both require conscious thought, the effective I.Q. drops sharply. A Harvard MBA drops to the level of an eighth grade student.[6]

Reduce Uncertainty

The worry about what may happen is often more stressful than after the event occurs. If you feel stressed out about a possible future problem, try to reduce the uncertainty around it. For example, if you are worried about a medical situation, find out as much as you can, including how you can cope with the condition. However, if you are not worried about a potential issue, then a focus on it could serve to increase your stress level.

A study with Huntington's Disease showed the effectiveness or reducing uncertainty. It is an incurable genetic disease that typically strikes in middle age. It starts with involuntary shaking and progresses to dementia and death. It is the disease that killed singing legend Woody Guthrie. If your parent has the disease, you have a 50% chance of inheriting it.

When a blood test was developed to determine if a person carried this disease, young adults who had a parent with the disease were given a choice to find out if they carried the defective gene. A research study found that after a six-month period, the average stress and happiness levels of those told that they would get the disease was the same as those that were disease free. Even more striking is the finding around those who declined to take the test and continued to worry from the uncertainty provoked stress. After six months, their average happiness level was significantly lower than the group that knew for certain that they would get the disease.[7]

Exercise

Virtually any form of exercise reduces your stress and causes the release of endorphins in the brain. Endorphins are the chemicals associated with the runner's high, but this good feeling is not specific to running. So be active in whatever form of exercise you enjoy. In light of the many benefits we get from physical activity, it is a good idea to develop the habit of exercising.

Ask for Help

We tend to want to do a job ourselves so that we are comfortable with the quality of the work. Also, our reluctance to let go often indicates an element of uncertainty. God created us to work together and help each other. Look for ways to work with others.

Sometimes, we need to delegate. It is often a mistake to take on too much and then feel overwhelmed. Jesus delegated to the twelve apostles. Do not let your issues of perfectionism or insecurity stop you from asking others to help.

Get Out into Nature

While it is not practical for all of us to live in a cabin in the woods, studies show that we are happier when we relate to nature. "At daybreak, Jesus went off to a solitary place" (Luke 4:42). Jesus often went off into the mountains or into the desert.

When we get out and admire God's creation, our minds are calmed. It is generally acknowledged that going for a walk is a good stress break. Not so well known is that science has found that a ten-minute nature walk is significantly more relaxing than a ten-minute walk through city streets.[8]

Take a Break

We all need a break from time to time to refresh our minds. This includes short breaks during the day and vacation days where we get out and do something we enjoy. Even God rested on the seventh day of creation. And the Ten Commandments designate the Sabbath as a day of rest.

Many companies force employees to take vacations because they realize productivity drops when vacations are not taken. Recreation is part of the joyful life that the Bible instructs us to live. Our ability to love others drops dramatically when we feel overwhelmed.

Post-Traumatic Growth

Just as we all injure muscles from time to time, we can also injure our brains from stress. In some cases, our brains not only recover but post-traumatic growth also brings us enhanced spiritual and emotional development beyond where we were before the trauma. This does not mean that the trauma was good; rather it means that we may benefit from our suffering.

Attributes of Post-Traumatic Growth

Post-traumatic growth enhances the three natural priorities of the mind. With respect to the first priority of meeting basic needs, the growth leads to a deeper appreciation of life. A sense of increased personal strength may develop because when someone gets through the trauma, they assume that they can successfully overcome future difficulties.

Thinking clearly, the second natural priority of the mind, shows up in spiritual growth. Post-traumatic growth may leave the trauma victim feeling closer to God. On the secular side, there is also the recognition of new opportunities that were not appreciated before the trauma.

Finally, post-traumatic growth can bring an enhanced desire to help others, the third natural priority of the mind. We saw in Chapter 6 the health benefits this brings and in Chapter 7 the happiness benefits.

A scientific study showed recovery from trauma can bring the benefits of personal growth and better health. George Vaillant of Harvard University studied WWII veterans who had also been Harvard undergraduate students. These men filled out an extensive questionnaire and participated in an in-depth interview at the conclusion of the war. The follow-up process included filling out questionnaires every two years and taking mental and physical tests every five years starting at age 45. Fifty veterans who saw heavy combat were compared with 110 veterans who did not see combat.

Heavy combat is obviously traumatic. Of the 50 veterans who faced this trauma, about half showed signs of personal growth following the trauma. This was measured as a desire to mentor the next generation and give back to the community. So the study was effectively looking at three groups: a group that was traumatized by combat and showed personal growth, a group that was traumatized by combat and did not show personal growth and a group that was not traumatized by combat. The group who saw battle but didn't show personal growth drank significantly more alcohol and had greater mental and physical health problems than the non-combat group. However, the combat veterans who experienced the personal growth were less anxious, showed greater wisdom and had better health in old age than the third group who did not face combat.[9]

The Thought Patterns of Trauma

Trauma victims typically go through three difficult areas during their recovery. The first is dealing with the emotional distress and uncertainty of the trauma. Next, victims typically go over their life history and re-appraise some events and are remorseful about missed opportunities. Finally, trauma leads victims to question their fundamental beliefs and goals. So a great deal of soul searching during an emotional period in the victim's life. Growth from the experience is far from certain, as illustrated by the combat veterans who turned to alcohol in response to trauma.

Finding Growth through God

"We also glory in our sufferings, because we know that suffering produces perseverance, perseverance, character; and character, hope" (Romans 5:3-4). The hope that Paul talks about is evident in post-traumatic growth, both through enhanced spirituality and in the appreciation of secular opportunities. Yet, many trauma victims fail to achieve any post-traumatic growth. The solution to finding growth is to ask God for it as part of your recovery.

Science shows that Christians with faith have a much better chance of achieving post-traumatic growth than non-believers and that this growth can be significant.[10,11,12] It is important to involve God in your recovery as discussed in the previous section on trauma recovery.

Summary

We all face difficulties and encounter stress as a result. When the stress is so intense that we become estranged from one of the three natural priorities of the mind, then we may suffer from PTSD. Fortunately, God has given us many ways to effectively cope with the stress.

Independent evidence indicates that Christians cope better with stressful situations and have a better chance of experiencing post-traumatic growth following an extremely stressful event. So place your trust in God.

Many people find growth following serious stress and that growth turns out to be how we are designed in the image of God. There can be a sense of personal strength and deepened appreciation of life in the image of God the Father, a feeling of being closer to God in the image of Jesus and an enhanced desire to help others in the image of the Holy Spirit. When troubles strike us, we also have a growth opportunity.

CONCLUSION

"Jesus said to them, 'no one who has left home or wife or brothers or parents or children for the sake of the kingdom of God will fail to receive many times as much in this age and, in the age to come, eternal life'"

(Luke 18:29-30).

Scripture teaches that we are called to develop ourselves in the image of God and as we do so, we reap tremendous benefits in our daily lives. Even if you question the accuracy of the Bible, the scientific evidence of its teaching demonstrates that it suggests a lifestyle that is more successful, meaningful, happier and healthier than the secular lifestyle. It also sets us up for better personal growth, easier self-motivation and greater capacity to deal with stress.

The greatest commandment calls on us to love God, not with the idea that we seek to repay God for His many blessings, but in the sense of a child wanting to emulate his or her parents. We are called to a love so strong that our personal development in His image dominates both our conscious minds and our hearts. Our identity centers on being a child of God maturing in His image.

Meaning of the Image of God

Based on the Scriptural understanding from Augustine, we are created in the image of the Trinity. This means we are created in the image of God the Father to create our own accomplishments according to His purpose and to meet our basic needs that protect our life. In the image of Jesus, we seek clear thought and understanding. And in the image of the Holy Spirit we are drawn to love others.

This understanding of being created in the image of God is useful in our daily lives in enhancing our happiness, our motivation and our development of post-traumatic growth. It is also evident in trauma symptoms, the meaning of humility and the spiritual illusions. It fits too well to be considered a coincidence.

Identity Controls our Heart

Multiple scientific studies show we act according to the identity we associate with ourselves, even when we do not realize why we go off in certain directions. This is because most of our thoughts take place in our hearts beyond our conscious recognition. We have seen how billion dollar programs cause more harm than good when participants are labeled as potential criminals or potential drug abusers. We have also seen positive results that exceed expectations when the participants are labeled good or valuable.

The Bible teaches us to adopt an identity as a righteous person, so we must learn to accept this positive identity. We know that we are not perfect, but should think of ourselves as maturing according to God's timeline. If we label ourselves as sinners, it will cause us to sin more.

Our identity as a child of God includes surrendering our lives to Jesus. This does not mean a life of sacrifice where we are passive slaves to God. The reality is we are simply living the way we were designed to live, while retaining our free will, our personal preferences and thoughts.

Importance of Humility in the Image of God

Humility is a vital virtue in the Christian lifestyle, yet it is frequently given a wrong or incomplete meaning. Scriptures calls on us not to compare ourselves with others, to keep an open mind and to serve. There is a positive role for pride in our lives as long as it does not interfere with any of these three aspects of humility.

The Tools of Satan

Satan seeks to trick us with a great lie and three illusions. The great lie is that humility means thinking less of ourselves. This leads us away from the identity we are called to adopt and distracts us from working on the true meaning of humility.

The selfish illusion tempts us to sin because we think it will make us happier. When these temptations are analyzed scientifically, we realize that we can't increase our overall happiness level through sin. Temptations are easier to resist when we recognize that they are illusions attractively packaged to fool us.

The control illusion is that our intellect controls what we do. A surprising and quite uncomfortable scientific finding is the extent to which our identity controls our behavior without our intellect realizing what is happening. The attitude we carry in our unconscious minds is what really counts.

Finally, the reward illusion prompts us to try to earn our salvation. If we view God as someone we seek to be fair to, then we distort who God is and what he wants from us. This distortion leads us to think God cares more about our actions than our acceptance, love and dependence.

Spiritual warfare

There is a spiritual battle in your heart. On one side are the gifts of love, joy and peace from the Holy Spirit. On the other are the great lie and the three spiritual illusions. You have the free will to choose, but it is easy to be tricked.

"Keeping a close watch on Him, they sent spies, who pretended to be sincere. They hoped to catch Jesus in something He said, so that they might hand Him over to the power and authority of the governor. So the spies questioned Him: 'Teacher, we know that you speak and teach what is right, and that you do not show partiality but teach the way of God in accordance with the truth. Is it right for us to pay taxes to Caesar or not?' He saw through the duplicity and said to them, 'Show me a denarius. Whose image and inscription are on it?' 'Caesar's' they replied. He said to them, 'Then give back to Caesar what is Caesar's, and to God what is God's'" (Luke 20:20-25).

We can control our hearts by choosing our identities. Whose image is on your heart?

ACKNOWLEDGEMENTS

First, I would like to acknowledge the inspiration, support and editing from my wife, Brenda. Without her, this book would not have been possible.

Writing the book has been a four-year journey with many people helping along the way. I would like to recognize Adam Babineau, Martin Bruin, Alan Carpen, Edmundo Contreras, Michael Dopp, Martin Epps, Derek Foster, John Frogley, Paul Hession, Ray Hession, Blaine Knapp, Nancy Lennox, Clyde MacDonald, Ron Mostrey, Brian MacGregor, John Morris, Kitti Murray, Edmin Omorogbe, Hans Prang, Keaton Robbins, Stephen Rolston, David Tessier, John Westbrook, Glen Williams, Irene Williams, Daniel Winter and Kari Yli-Renko.

I would also like to give credit to V.J. Suresh for the cover design, Donald Marsanic for the book formatting and to those whose work forms the basis for the book. On the theology side, the book draws heavily on the writings of Augustine of Hippo and of C.S. Lewis. Mihaly Csikszentmihalyi, Edward Deci, Dacher Keltner, Stephen Post, Richard Ryan, Martin Seligman and Timothy Wilson are the main scientists upon whose work I have relied. Of course, I am responsible for any errors.

To all of you, a very sincere thank you.

NOTES

Introduction – The Great Social Experiment

1. McCord, Joan, "Cures that harm: Unanticipated outcomes of crime prevention programs," *Annals of the American Academy of Political and Social Science*

2. Wilson, Timothy D, *Redirect: The Surprising New Science of Psychological Change* (New York: Little Brown and Company 2011)

3. Lewis, CS *The Weight of Glory* (New York: Harper Collins 2001)

4. Lewis, CS *Surprised by Joy: The shape of my early life* (London, UK: Geoffrey Bles 1955)

Chapter One – Love God

1. Piper, John *Desiring God* (Sisters, Oregon: Multnomah Publishers 1986)

2. Emory J and B Waugh, *The Works of John Wesley A.M.*, Sermon #73 (New York: Methodist Episcopal Church, J Collard Printer 1831)

3. Mathesius, Johannes, *The Table Talk of Martin Luther* (Eisleben, Germany: 1566)

4. Calvin, John, Institutes of the Christian Religion translated by John Allen (Philadelphia: Presbyterian Board of Publication 1813)

5. McDonald, Nicholas "34 Books that Influenced C.S. Lewis" http://scribblepreach.com/2013/04/09/34-books-that-influenced-c-s-lewis/ (Posted April 9, 2013)

6. Pope John Paul II, *Apostolic Letter Augustinum Hipposensem* (Vatican August 28, 1986)

7. Augustine of Hippo, *Confessions, Book* 10, Chapter 27, Paragraph 38

8. Hill, Edmund commenting in *The Works of St. Augustine* (New York: Augustinian Heritage Institute 1991)

9. Augustine of Hippo *On the Trinity,* Book 7, Chapter 6, Paragraph 12

10. Augustine of Hippo *On the Trinity,* Book 15, Chapter 20, Paragraph 39

11. Augustine of Hippo *On the Trinity,* Book 9, Chapter 12, Paragraph 17

12. Field T, M Hernandez-Reif, O Quintino, S Schamberg and C Kuhn, "Elder Retired Volunteers Benefit from Giving Massage Therapy to Infants," *Journal of Applied Gerontology* 1998, 17:229-239

13. Augustine of Hippo *On the Trinity,* Book 15, Chapter 17, Paragraph 29

14. Augustine of Hippo *On the Trinity,* Book 15, Chapter 19, Paragraph 37

15. Augustine of Hippo *On the Trinity,* Book 15, Chapter 19, Paragraph 37

16. Augustine of Hippo *On the Trinity,* Book 15, Chapter 17, Paragraph 27

Chapter Two – Accept the Glory

1. Edelman, Benjamin, "Red Light States: Who Buys Online Adult Entertainment" *Journal of Economic Perspectives* 2009: 23:209-220

2. MacInnis, Cara and Gordon Hodson, "Do American States with More Religious or Conservative Populations Search More for Sexual Content on Google?" *Archives of Sexual Behavior* 2015, 44:137-147

3. Chalmers, Thomas, *The Expulsive Power of a New Affection* (Minneapolis, Curiosmith 2012)

4. Petrosino, A, C Turpin-Petrosino and JO Fincenauer, "Well-meaning programs can have harmful effects! Lessons from experiments of programs such as scared straight," *Crime and Delinquency* 2000, 46: 354-379

5. Wilson, Timothy D, *Redirect: The Surprising New Science of Psychological Change* (New York: Little Brown and Company 2011)

6. US General Accounting Office, *Youth illicit drug use prevention: DARE long-term evaluations and federal efforts to identify effect programs Report GAO-03-172R* (Washington DC, US Government Printing Office 2003)

7. D.A.R.E program website www.dare.com

8. Carlier, IVE, AE Voerman and BPR Gersons, "The influence of occupational debriefing on post-traumatic stress symptomatology in traumatized police officers," *British Journal of Medical Psychology* 2000, 73: 87-98

9. McCord, J, "A thirty-year follow-up of treatment effects," *American Psychologist* 1978, 33: 284-289

10. Olds, D L, "The nurse-family partnership: An evidence-based preventative intervention," *Infant Mental Health Journal* 2006, 27: 5-25

11. Bisagno, John, *The Power of Positive Praying* (Grand Rapids, Michigan: Zondervan 1965)

12. Graham, Billy, *The Holy Spirit, Activating God's Power in Your Life* (New York: Thomas Nelson 1978)

13. Lepper, M R, "Dissonance, self-perception and honesty in children," *Journal of Personality and Social Psychology* 1973, 25: 65-74

14. Wilson, T D, and G D Lassiter, "Increasing intrinsic interest with superfluous extrinsic constraints," *Journal of Personality and Social Psychology* 1982, 42: 811-819

15. Yeung, N and C von Hippel, "Stereotype threat increases the likelihood that female drivers in a simulator run over jaywalkers," *Accident Analysis and Prevention* 2008, 40: 667-674

16. Kane, J M, and J E Mertz, "Debunking myths about gender and mathematics performance," *Notices of the American Mathematical Society* 2012, 59(1): 10-21

17. Walton, G M, and G L Cohen, "Stereotype lift," *Journal of Experimental Social Psychology* 2003, 39:456-467

18. Wilson, Timothy D, *Redirect: The Surprising New Science of Psychological Change* (New York: Little Brown and Company 2011)

19. Levy, BR, C Pilver, PH Chung and MD Slade, "Subliminal Strengthening: Improving Older Individuals' Physical Function Over Time With an Implicit-Age-Stereotype Intervention" *Psychological Science* 1014, 25:2127-2135

Chapter Three – Satan's Great Deception

1. Augustine of Hippo *City of God,* Book 14, Chapter 13

2. Lewis, C.S., *The Screwtape Letters,* Number 14 (London: Geoffrey Bles 1942)

3. Piff, P, DM Stancato, S Cote, R Mendoza-Denton and D Keltner, "Higher social class predicts increased unethical behavior" *Proceedings of the National Academy of Sciences* February 28, 2012 109(9)

4. Collins, Jim, *Good to Great: Why Some Companies Make the Leap ... and Others Don't* (New York: Harper Collins, 1997)

5. Chapman, Gary, *The Five Love Languages: How to Express Heartfelt Commitment to Your Mate* (Chicago: Moody Publishers 1992) Note – This story is not found in later editions of his book.

6. Lewis, C.S., *Mere Christianity* (London: Geoffrey Bles 1952)

7. Warren, Rick, *The Purpose Driven Life* (Grand Rapids, Michigan: Zondervan 2002)

Chapter Four – The Three Powerful Spiritual Illusions

1. Mick, I, P Stokes, D Erritzoe, A Colasanti, H Bowden-Jones, L Clark, R Gunn, E Rabiner, G Searle, D Nutt and A Lingford-Hughes "Endogenous Opioid Release in Pathological Gamblers After an Oral Amphetamine Challenge: A [^{11}C] Carfentanil Pet Study" *European Neuropsychopharmacology* 2014, 24(2): 8699-8700

2. Mauss, IB, M Tamir, CL Anderson and NS Savino, "Can Seeking Happiness Make People Happy? Paradoxical Effects of Valuing Happiness" *Emotion* 2011, 11(4): 807-815

3. Augustine of Hippo *Confessions* Book 8, Chapter 9

4. Darwin, Charles, *The Expressions of the Emotions in Man and Animals with Photographic and Other Illustrations* (London: J Murray, 1872)

5. Augustine of Hippo *Against Julian* Book 6, Chapter 15

6. Monroe, KR, "The roots of moral courage" *Greater Good – The Science of a Meaningful Life* June 22, 2010

Chapter Five – A Life Full of Success

1. Wang Q and X Lin "Does Religious Beliefs Affect Economic Growth? Evidence from provincial-level panel data in China" *China Economic Review* 2014 31:277-287

2. Cameron, C. Daryl and Barbara Fredrickson "Mindfulness Facets Predict Helping Behavior and Distinct Helping-Related Emotions" *Mindfulness* January 6, 2015

3. Graham, Billy, *Just As I Am: The Autobiography of Billy Graham* (New York: Harper Collins 1997)

4. Thomas, Gary, *Sacred Pathways: Discover your soul's path to God* (Grand Rapids, Michigan: Zondervan 2010)

5. Pope John Paul II, *Apostolic Letter Augustinum Hipposensem* (Vatican August 28, 1986)

Chapter Six – Think Like Jesus

1. Seligman, Martin *Flourish: A visionary and new understanding of happiness and well-being* (New York: Free Press 2011)

2. Wilson, Timothy D, *Strangers to Ourselves: Discovering the Adaptive Unconscious* (Cambridge, Ma: Belknap Press 2002)

3. Csikszentmihalyi, Mihaly *Flow: The Psychology of Optimal Experience* (New York: Harper and Row 1990)

4. Wilson, T, D Reinhard, E Westgate, D Gilbert, N Ellerbeck, C Hahn, C Brown and A Shaked "Just Think: The challenges of the disengaged mind" *Science* 2014 345(6192): 75-77

5. Lewis, C.S., *Mere Christianity* (London: Geoffrey Bles 1952)

6. Augustine of Hippo *On Christian Doctrine*, Book 4, Chapter 5, Paragraph 7

7. Augustine of Hippo *On Christian Doctrine*, Book 2, Chapter 6, Paragraph 7

8. Augustine of Hippo *Confessions*, Book 3, Chapter 5, Paragraph 9

9. Augustine of Hippo *The Literal Meaning of Genesis*, Book 1, Chapter 18, Paragraph 37

10. Augustine of Hippo *On Christian Doctrine*, Book 3, Chapter 5, Paragraph 9

11. Augustine of Hippo *City of God*, Book 6, Chapter 6

12. Augustine of Hippo *On Genesis*, Book 2, Chapter 9, Paragraph 20

13. Beck, Richard "The Bait and Switch of Contemporary Christianity" from his website Experimental Theology posted August .8, 2009: http://experimentaltheology.blogspot.ca /2009/08/bait-and-switch-of-contemporary.html

14. Lewis, C.S., *Reflection on the Psalms* (Boston, Ma: Houghton Mifflin Harcourt 1964)

15. Peale, Norman Vincent, *The Power of Positive Thinking* (Englewood NJ: Prentice Hall 1952)

16. Duffin, Jacalyn, *Medical Miracles: Doctors, Saints and Healing in the Modern World* (New York: Oxford University Press 2008)

17. Ortberg, John, *Who Is This Man?* (Grand Rapids, Michigan: Zondervan 2012)

18. Pope Francis *Encyclical Letter Laudato si* (Vatican June 18, 2015)

19. Wesley, John, *A Plain Account of Christian* (Peabody, Massachusetts: Hendrickson Publishers Inc. 2007) – taken from The Works of John Wesley edited by Thomas Jackson 1872

Chapter Seven – The Fire of the Holy Spirit

1. Cameron, CD and BL Fredrickson, "Mindfulness Facets Predict Helping Behavior and Distinct Helping-Related Emotions" *Mindfulness* Published Online January 6, 2015

2. Machiavelli, Niccolo, *Discourses on Livy* 1517

3. Gopnik, Alison, *The Philosophical Baby* (New York: Farrar, Straus and Giroux 2009)

4. Warneken, F and M Tomasello, "The roots of human altruism" *British Journal of Psychology* 2009, 100: 455-471

5. Keltner, Dacher (editor), Jeremy Adam Smith (editor) and Jason March (editor), *The Compassion Instinct: The Science of Human Goodness* (New York: WW Norton 2010)

6. Keltner, D "The compassion instinct", *Greater Good – The Science of a Meaningful Life* Spring 2004

7. Castiello, U, C Becchio, S Zoia, C Nelini, L Sartori, L Blason, G D'Ottavio, M Bulgheroni and V Gallese, "Wired to be social: The ontology of human interaction," *PLoS ONE* 2010, 5(10): e13199

8. Kohn, A, "Beyond selfishness," *Psychology Today* October 1988

9. Hamlin, JK, K Wynn and P Bloom, "Social evaluation by preverbal infants," *Nature* 2007, 450: 557-559

10. Liszkowski, U, M Carpenter and M Tomasello, "Twelve-month-olds communicate helpfully and appropriately for knowledgeable and ignorant partners," *Cognition* 2008, 108: 732-739

11. Tomasello, Michael, *Why We Cooperate* (Cambridge, MA: MIT Press 2009)

12. Aknin, L, JK Hamlin and EW Dunn "Giving Leads to Happiness in Young Children" *PLoS ONE* 2012 7(6): e39211

13. Warneken, F, K Lohse, A Melis and M Tomasello, "Young children share the spoils after collaboration," *Psychological Science* 2011 22(2): 267-273

14. Saxe, Rebecca presentation at TED July 2009. It can be found at: http://www.ted.com/talks/lang/en/rebecca_saxe_how_brains_make_moral_judgments.html

15. Lewis, C.S. *The Problem of Pain* (San Francisco: Harper Collins 1940)

16. Rilling, JK, DA Gutman, TR Zeh, G Pagnoni, G Berns and C Kilts "A Neural Basis for Social Cooperation" *Neuron* 2002 35:395-405

17. Wheeler, ME and ST Fiske "Controlling Racial Prejudice: Social-congitive goals affect t amygdala and stereotype activation" *Psychological Science* 2005 16(1): 56-63

18. Lyubomirsky, S, L King and E Diener, "The benefits of frequent positive affect: Does happiness lead to success?" *Bulletin of the American Psychological Association* 2005 3(6): 803-855

19. Abel, E and M Kruger "Smile Intensity in Photographs Predicts Longevity" *Psychological Science* Published online February 28, 2010 1177/0956797610363775

20. Harker, L and D Keltner "Expressions of positive emotion in women's college yearbook pictures and their relationship to personality and life outcomes across adulthood" *Journal of Personality and Social Psychology* 2011 80: 112-124

21. Marmot MG, GD Smith, S Stansfeld, C Patel, F North, J Head, I White, E Brunner and A Feeney, "Health inequalities among British civil servants: The Whitehall II study" *The Lancet* 1991; 337:1397-93

22. Porath, CL, A Gerbesi, and S Schoroh, "The Effects of Civility on Advice, Leadership, and Performance" *Journal of Applied Physiology* posted online March 23, 2015

23. Porath CL and A Erez 'Does Rudeness Really Matter: The effects of rudeness on task performance and helpfulness" *The Academy of Management Journal* 2007 50(5): 1181-1197

24. Emmonds, Robert, *Thanks!: How Practicing Gratitude Can Make You Happier* (New York: Mariner Books 2008)

25. Mills, PJ, L Redwine, K Wilson, Meredith, A Pung, K Chinh, B Greenberg, O Lunde, A Maisel, A Raisinghani, A Wood and D Chopra "The role of gratitude in spiritual well-being in asymptomatic heart failure patients" *Spirituality and Clinical Practice* 2015 2(1): 5-17

26. Keltner, Dacher, *Born to Be Good: The Science of a Meaningful Life* (New York: WW Norton 2009)

27. App, B, DN McIntosh, CL Reed and MJ Hertenstein, "Is love best expressed through a touch or a smile," *Emotion* 2011, 11(3): 603-617

28. Csikszentmihalyi, Mihaly, *Finding Flow: The Psychology of Engagement with Everyday Life* (New York: Harper Collins, 2001)

29. Cohen S, D Janicki-Deverts, R Turner and W Doyle, "Does Hugging Provide Stress-Buffering Social Support? A Study of Susceptibility to Upper Respiratory Infection and Illness" *Psychological Science* 2015 26:135-147

30. Field, T, M Diego and M Hernandez-Reif, "Preterm infant massage therapy research: a review," *Infant Behavior and Development* 2010, 33(2): 115-124

31. Enright, Robert, *Forgiveness Is a Choice: A Step-By-Step Process for Resolving Anger and Restoring Hope* (Washington DC: American Psychological Association 2001)

32. Krause, N and CG Ellison, "Forgiveness by God, forgiveness by others, and psychological well-being in late life." *Journal for the Scientific Study of Religion* 2003, 42: 77-93

33. Schumann, K, J Zaki and C Dweck, "Addressing the empathy deficit: Beliefs about the malleability of empathy predict effortful responses when empathy is challenging" *Journal of Personality and Social Psychology* 2014, 107(3): 475-493

34. Rizzolatti G and M Fabbri-Destro, "Mirror Neurons: From Discovery to Autism," *Experimental Brain Research* 2010, 200:223-237

35. Post, Stephen and Jill Neimark, *Why Good Things Happen to Good People: How to Live a Longer, Healthier, Happier Life by the Simple Act of Giving* (New York: Broadway Books 2007)

36. Schwartz, C and M Sendor, "Helping others helps oneself: Response shift effects in peer support," *Social Science and Medicine* 1999, 48(11): 1563-1575

37. Scott, B, J Colquitt, EL Paddock and T Judge, "A Daily Investigation of the Role of Manager Empathy on Employee Well-Being," *Organizational Behavior and Human Decision Processes* 2010 113(2): 127-140

38. Spiegel, D, JR Bloom, HC Kraemer and E Gottheil, "Effect of psychosocial treatment on survival of cancer patients with metastatic breast cancer," *The Lancet* 1989, 2:888-890

39. Post, Stephen and Jill Neimark, *Why Good Things Happen to Good People: How to Live a Longer, Healthier, Happier Life by the Simple Act of Giving* (New York: Broadway Books 2007)

40. Ayan, S, "Laughing matters," *Scientific American Mind* 2009 20(2): 24-31

41. Klein, Amelia, *Humor in Children's Lives: A Guidebook for Practitioners* (Santa Barbara: Praeger 2003)

42. Titze, M, "The dadaistic roots of therapeutic humor" *Humor and Health Journal* 2006 15(1)

Chapter Eight – How to Be Joyful Always

1. Fredrickson, BL, K Grewen, K Coffee, S Algoe, AM Firestine, JMG Arevalo, J Ma and S Cole "A functional genomic perspective on human well-being" *Proceedings of the National Academy of Sciences* 2013, 110(33): 13684-13689

2. Search of Amazon website with the term happiness: http://www.amazon.com

3. Gibbons, John, *I Can't Get No...Job Satisfaction: That Is*, (New York: The Conference Board 2010, Publication Number R-1459-09-RR)

4. Stevenson, B and J Wolfers, "The paradox of declining female," *American Economic Journal: Economic Policy* 2009, 1(2): 190-225

5. Seligman, Martin presentation at TED February 2004. It can be found at: http://www.ted.com/talks/martin_seligman_on_the_state_of_psychology.html

6. ibid

7. Brickman P, D Coates and R Janoff-Bulman, "Lottery winners and accident victims: Is happiness relative?" *Journal of Personality and Social Psychology* 1078, 36(8): 917-927

8. Killingsworth, M and D Gilbert, "A Wandering Mind is an Unhappy Mind," *Science* 2010, 330(6006): 932

9. Wilcox, W Bradford (editor), *The State of our Unions: Marriage in America 2011* (Charlottesville, VA: Institute for American Values/National Marriage Project 2011)

10. Robbins, J, "The economics of happiness" *Greater Good – The Science of a Meaningful Life* July 20, 2010

11. ibid

12. Krieger, Lawrence S and Kennon M Sheldon, "What makes lawyers happy? A data-driven prescription to redefine professional success" *The George Washington Law Review* 2015 83(2): 554-627

13. Gilbert, DT and TD Wilson, "Prospection: experiencing the future," *Science* 317: 1351-1354

14. Ayan, S, "Laughing matters," *Scientific American Mind* 2009 20(2): 24-31

15. Danner DD, DA Snowdon and WV Friessen, "Positive emotions in early life and longevity: Findings for the Nun Study," *Journal of Personality and Social Psychology* 2001, 80(5): 804-813

16. Vujicic, Nick, *Life Without Limits: Inspiration for a ridiculously good life* (New York: Doubleday 2010)

17. Diensbier, RA, D Hillman, J Lehnhoff, J Hillman and MC Valkenaar, "An emotion-attribution approach to moral behavior: Interfacing cognitive and avoidance theories of moral development" *Psychological Review* 1975 82:299-315

Chapter Nine – Motivation in the Image of God

1. Lehrer, Jonah, *How We Decide* (Boston: Houghton Mifflin Harcourt 2009)

2. Ariely, D, U Gneezy, G Lowenstein and N Mayer, "Large Stakes and Big Mistakes," *Review of Economic Studies* 2009 76(2): 451-469

3. Harlow, HF, MK Harlow and D Meyer, "Learning Motivation by a Manipulation Drive," *Journal of Experimental Psychology* 1950, 40: 228-234

4. Glucksberg, S, "The Influence of Strength and Drive on Functional Fixedness and Perceptual Recognition," *Journal of Experimental Psychology* 1962, 63:36-41

5. Mellstrom, C and M Johannesson "Crowing Out in Blood Donations, Was Titmus Right?" *Journal of the European Economic Association* June 2008 6(4): 845-863

6. Gneezy, U and A Rustichini, "A Fine is a Price," *Journal of Legal Studies* January 2000 29(1): 1-18

7. Bowles, Sam, *Machiavelli's Mistake: Why Good Incentives Are No Substitute for Good Citizens,* presentation to the London School of Economics on June 30, 2009

8. Geraci, A and L Surian "The developmental roots of fairness: infants' reactions to equal and unequal distributions of resources" *Developmental Science* 2011, 14 (5): 1012-1020

9. Pink, Daniel *Drive: The Surprising Truth About What Motivates Us* (New York: Riverhead Books 2009)

10. Rath, Tom *Are Your Fully Charged: The 3 Keys to Energizing Your Work and Life* (San Francisco: Silicon Guild 2015)

11. Graham, Billy *Nearing Home: Life, Faith and Finishing Well* (Nashville: Thomas Nelson 2011)

Chapter Ten – Find God Through Your Troubles

1. Scaer, Robert, *The Body Bears the Burden: Trauma, Disassociation and Disease* (Binghamton, NY: Haworth Medical Press 2001)

2. Sapolsky, R, "Glucocorticoids and hippocampal atrophy in neuropsychiatric disorders," *Archives of General Psychiatry* 2000, 57: 925-935

3. Ganzel, B, BJ Casey, G Gloves, HU Voss, E Temple, "The Aftermath of 9/11: Effect of intensity and recentcy of trauma on outcome," *Emotion* 2007, 7(2):227-238

4. Hillenbrand, Laura, *Unbroken: A World War II Story of Survival, Resilience and Redemption* (New York: Random House 2010)

5. Selver, LJ, TE Ziegler and SD Pollak, "Social Vocalizations Can Release Oxytocin in Humans," *Proceedings of the Royal Society B* published online May 12, 2010

6. Rock, David, *Your Brain at Work: Strategies for Overcoming Distraction, Regaining Focus and Working Smarter All Day Long* (New York: Harper Collins 2009)

7. Wiggins, S, P Whyte, M Higgins, S Adam, J Theilmann, M Bloch, SB Sheps, MT Schechter and MR Hayden, The psychological of predictive testing for Huntington's Disease," *The New England Journal of Medicine* 1992, 327:1401-1405

8. Nisbet, EK, JM Zelinski and SA Murphy, "Happiness is in Our Nature: Exploring Nature Relatedness as a Contributor

to Subjective Well-Being," *Journal of Happiness Studies* 2011, 12(2): 303-322

9. Ardelt, M, SD Landes and GE Vaillant "The long-term effects of World War II combat exposure on later life well-being moderated by generativity," *Research in Human Development* 2010. *7*(3), 202-220

10. Emmons, RA, PM Colby and HA Kaiser, "When losses lead to gains: Personal goals and the recovery of meaning," In PTP Wong and PS Fry (editors), *The Human Quest for Meaning: A Handbook of Psychological Research and Clinical Application* (Mahwah, NJ: Lawrence Erlbaum 1998)

11. Parapully, J, R Rosenbaum, L Van den Daele and E Nzewi, "Thriving After Trauma: The experience of parents of murdered children," *Journal of Humanistic Psychology* 42:33-70.

12. Park, CL, LH Cohen and R Murch, "Assessment and prediction of stress-related growth" *Journal of Personality* 1996, 64:71-105

INDEX

ABOUT THE AUTHOR

John Brooks is a former business executive who was VP at CIBC Wood Gundy. He has also served as CEO of various entrepreneurial companies and was named Ottawa Entrepreneur of the Year. He is a Chartered Financial Analyst and also holds a Masters degree in Physiology.

John lives in Ottawa, Canada with his wife Brenda. They have 4 grown children and 7 grandchildren.

Printed in March 2016
by Gauvin Press,
Gatineau, Québec